BOXING

BY

R. G. ALLANSON-WINN
B.A. CANTAB.

ILLUSTRATED

Edited by B. Fletcher Robinson

1897

THIS TREATISE ON THE

NOBLE ART

IS AFFECTIONATELY DEDICATED

TO MY COUSIN AND BROTHER BRUISER

Charles, Lord Headley

AS A SLIGHT MARK OF MY APPRECIATION OF HIS MANLY

INSTINCTS AND LOVE OF ALL TRUE SPORT.

AUTHOR'S PREFACE.

IT must be satisfactory to all true lovers of the Art, as a national and progressive institution, to feel that the past few years have witnessed changes—mostly in the right direction—in the science of Boxing. First principles have not indeed changed, but the correct application of those principles has made a considerable step forward and is better understood. There has been no stagnation, and healthy Englishmen cannot but feel the greatest satisfaction that this branch of Athletics is daily gaining ground and increasing in popularity in all classes of the community.

In a former treatise the author of the following pages endeavoured to put beginners into the way of learning from first principles; in the present work an attempt is made to go rather more fully into the subject, and, with this object in view, he has added to certain chapters authentic accounts of important fights in which occurred situations or incidents especially dealt with in those chapters.

It is hoped that by this means the volume may not only be rendered more readable, but that more attention may be drawn to the various distinctive styles and the strong and weak points of fighters of different years.

Discussion or digression on points of ancient history are here avoided as being unnecessary in a practical work. Castor and Pollux do not interest us much; the heavy cestus wielded by Milo must have made the wearer very slow, and, could the redoubtable champion of Cortona be now brought to the scratch in all his pristine vigour and armament, he would probably make but a poor show against a Peter Jackson, a Corbett, or a Fitzsimmons.

In the chapter set aside for the purpose reference is made to the comparative merits of certain pugilists, though it is impossible to truly estimate, from the contemplation of any particular fight, what such and such a man would do if opposed to a fighter of quite another school and style. Such discussion must be regarded as speculative to a very great extent. It is, however, always interesting to speculate on possibilities even though hampered with such intricate questions as comparative intelligence, condition, style, speed and reach, so long as *some* good is gleaned from the speculation.

Of recent years playing for the "knock out" has been much in vogue amongst professionals and amateurs alike, and, as it appears open to question whether this plan of campaign is to be commended or not, as favourable to the advancement of the science, some consideration of the subject in Chapter IX. has seemed advisable.

It has also been thought well to indicate some of the more prominent qualifications which go towards furnishing the raw material, as the author has occasionally been pained by noticing amongst his friends men who were pre-eminently fitted for the work by nature but who, not recognizing the fact, have never taken the trouble to learn.

It is often hard, when writing on technical subjects, to avoid ambiguities and repetitions, but an attempt has been made in the following pages to be as clear and concise as possible, as well as to bring the book well up to date.

It is to be regretted that want of space precludes

the possibility of quoting a larger number of the more celebrated prize-fights. Those selected have been picked out with some care from a very large batch of descriptions, and, of necessity, the doughty deeds of many mighty punishment-takers of the old school are missing from the present short record. In order to make up for this to some extent, and to facilitate a reference to really interesting accounts of the older battles of the ring, a list of the Champions of England is given at the end of the book, and full descriptions of the fights may be perused in the pages of *Pugilistica* and *Boxiana*.

For descriptions of modern glove-fights the reader is referred to the back numbers of the various sporting papers, and these can usually be obtained at the offices of those papers.

It will then be borne in mind that this volume is merely a handbook on the subject of boxing and fighting: the few descriptions of prize-fights have been collated as aids to assist students in their efforts to attain a thorough theoretical as well as practical knowledge of the subject. Possibly the very best examples have not been selected, but it is hoped that excuses will be made if this is the case, since the field of selection is so very large.

CONTENTS.

CHAPTER		PAGE
I.	INTRODUCTION	13
II.	POSITION AND STYLE	25
III.	LEG WORK	36
IV.	STRAIGHT HITTING	57
V.	HALF-ARM OR ROUND HITS	109
VI.	GUARDING AND STOPPING	142
VII.	THE 'SIDE-STEP' AND 'SLIPPING'	178
VIII.	TIMING AND COUNTERING	192
IX.	THE CROSS-COUNTER AND KNOCK-OUT BLOWS	199
X.	RIGHT-HANDED BOXERS	207
XI.	FEINTS	210
XII.	FOUL PLAY	216
XIII.	WEAK POINTS AND DANGEROUS HITS	253
XIV.	NATURAL FIGHTERS	260
XV.	COMPARISONS AND QUALIFICATIONS	265
XVI.	INSTRUCTION AND TRAINING	308
XVII.	CATCHES, FALLS, AND IN-FIGHTING	324
XVIII.	BAD EXAMPLES	343
XIX.	LA SAVATE	346
XX.	DEFINITIONS AND RULES	356
XXI.	SUMMARY OF MAXIMS	379
	APPENDIX	383

LIST OF PLATES.

1. POSITION	*Frontispiece*	
2. GETTING OUT OF REACH	*To face page*	41
3. LEAD WITH LEFT, TOES STRAIGHT, HIT STRAIGHT	,, ,,	57
4. LEAD WITH LEFT, TOE TURNED IN, HIT PULLED ACROSS	,, ,,	61
5. GUARD FOR RIGHT-HAND HIT AT BODY	,, ,,	109
6. DUCK TO RIGHT, WITH BODY-BLOW	,, ,,	125
7. GUARD FOR MARK	,, ,,	143
8. GUARD FOR HEAD	,, ,,	145
9. THE SIDE-STEP	,, ,,	179
10. RIGHT-HANDED CROSS COUNTER, I	,, ,,	199
11. RIGHT-HANDED CROSS COUNTER, II	,, ,,	202
12. LEFT-HANDED CROSS COUNTER	,, ,,	206
13. STEP TO LEFT, WITH BODY-BLOW FOR RIGHT-HANDED MAN	,, ,,	209
14. SLIPPING	,, ,,	260
15. THE DRAW FOR CROSS COUNTER	,, ,,	303
16. CONTRACTED-ARM HIT	,, ,,	325
17. THE UPPER-CUT	,, ,,	329
18. IN-FIGHTING	,, ,,	333

BOXING.

CHAPTER I.

INTRODUCTION.

A WELL-DEVELOPED intelligence and power of seeing "the reason why" is of great utility in boxing. True it is that many men of small mental capacity fight right well *instinctively;* they are strong and quick, but their prowess is only on a level with the agility of the monkey, and they would do far better if they had brains and could *think* out the reason for every attack and every defence. We are really only superior to the brute creation in that we have brains and hands; in the matter of mere strength and quickness they are, bulk for bulk, immeasurably our superiors.

In the earliest contests between man and man, with only nature's weapons, the scratching and biting must have been terrific, and, if the *casus belli* were sufficiently important, possibly one or other had an eye gouged out or was ultimately strangled. Science now steps in and says—"Here is a plan by which the scratcher and biter is kept at a distance; it is not easy to learn, and it is quite contrary to your preconceived ideas; it consists in simply hitting your opponent sufficiently hard and in the right place with the naked fist. The scratcher will not only fail to reach you, but he will measure his length upon the ground. If he should get up you can repeat the process until he is tired of it." All this of course may seem very self-evident to the initiated, but it is by no means thoroughly understood or appreciated by the average man, who, without knowledge, thinks he can hold his own by brute force alone.

Not one man in a hundred, taking the population all round, has the faintest idea what straight and effective hitting really means, and many who do know are unable, from want of practice or other reasons, to bring their knowledge into play. It is somewhat irritating to meet with persons who say that a sound knowledge of boxing is of no use in a row. It is of the greatest value, for, if you have it, your hits are not wasted; you can measure distances with a practised eye. If you are about to be attacked one effective hit may settle everything, and strike terror into the heart of the assailant before he has even made up his mind how to begin. Then again you are in a position to successfully protect the weak and helpless, or to take the shine out of some blatant and offensive bully.

There are refined persons who contend with warmth and some truth that fighting has its brutal aspect. It no doubt seems, at first sight, cruel to break a man's jaw, knock out his teeth, or double him up with a well-tucked-in hit on the mark, but if he richly deserves such treatment, who has a right to complain? It is a great thing to feel confident that you are able to inflict the damage, and the feeling will not make you quarrelsome or brutal unless you are so by nature.

One of our most interesting modern writers of fiction has introduced a delightfully warlike knight —Sir Nigel Loring—into one of his recent works; but few persons reading the book can quite sympathize with the systematic manner in which the plucky little man, in his search for "honour," picks quarrels with even the most quiet gentlemen. Doubtless in those good old days there existed such men as Dr. Conan Doyle has depicted; at the present time his boxing prototype would never be out of prison, he would be a pest to society!

Again, it may be taken for granted that no man has ever reached the highest positions in the world of fisticuffs without having experienced many hard knocks; he has gone through the mill, and knows perfectly well what a chance blow will often do, and therefore he does not court a useless row. His science is for self-defence, and is not to be debased in a worthless cause.

In these days of many mouths to feed, difficulty of getting employment, and incessant necessity of rapid thought, brought about by the use of steam and electricity, it should be the object of every good citizen to get through life as smoothly as possible, and without delays and distractions of an unnecessary character; therefore—

> "Beware
> Of entrance to a quarrel; but, being in,
> Bear 't that the opposed may beware of thee."

But if the art of Boxing is useful as a means of self-defence, how much more is it to be prized as one of the finest known means of cultivating the qualities of patience and self-control? Patience is so necessary, that it may be doubted whether any boxer has ever reached the first rank without putting it into practice to a very large extent, and, if patience and self-control can be once inculcated, they may be of use to a man outside the ring and in all his relations with his fellow-man.

The buffets of an unsympathetic world can be borne with greater equanimity, and since the desired qualities are *mental* and governed by intelligence, there is no reason why they should not form a check to hereditary violence of temper and ill-humour. Even the enemies of boxing as a sport cannot deny its advantages in the matter of healthy exercise. The liver is kept in order, and there is bound to be a healthy skin action: it, however, always seems a pity that more boxing is not done in the open air. Severe exertion in crowded and ill-ventilated rooms may lead to a certain amount of congestion which would not be the case in the fresh country air.

The refinement of feeling which has prompted a certain class to object to boxing on account of its brutality has also led up to a further objection on the score of danger. We have, as a nation, always been addicted to field sports, and those sports, field or otherwise, into which the element of danger conspicuously enters have ever been the marked favourites with Britishers.

Most of us have observed amongst superior and sensitive persons a tendency to hesitate about taking a decided step in *any* direction; it is the fear of "giving themselves away." They dare not take a leap in the dark even though they know it to be *in the right direction*. But this is not the spirit which actuated the hardy Norsemen when they launched their poor little cockle-shells on the bleak North Sea; this is not the spirit of the Anglo-Saxon race which to-day rules the world.

From the time when Robin Hood and Little John contended with rough quarter-staves, to the day when Napoleon said, "Confound those English, they don't know when they are beaten," the tough, ingrained hardiness of the race has shown itself in innumerable ways and on all occasions, and we don't want to see any change just now.

Still, as a matter of fact, there is very little real danger in boxing. Permanent and serious injuries are extremely rare, and what is a black eye or broken nose, or the loss of a tooth, compared with the advantages to be gained?

Many other sports are far more dangerous—take, for example, football, polo, hunting, steeple-chasing, shooting. There are many thousands of men and boys who box, but very few comparatively

INTRODUCTION. 19

can afford to play polo; yet the accidents in the latter pastime are numerous and serious, whilst the percentage in the former is absurdly low, even if you throw in prize-fights.

All who hold my views find additional pleasure in the fact that so many of our fellow-creature can join in a sport which is, according to our own lights, one of the best obtainable. In no other game or sport can a man get so much hard exercise into such a short space of time. It is very inexpensive, it brings all classes together, and there is hardly a spot on this earth where the British colour flies where a set of boxing-gloves is not to be found.

To become a good boxer or fighter it is not necessary to be a spectator at sanguinary prize-fights; though as regards the brutalizing effect of such exhibitions, one cannot help recognizing the fact that the combatants are free agents of an age to appreciate the risks they run.

In the case of bull-fights, etc., dumb creatures are tortured for man's amusement, and *here* the brutalizing effect may be seen at once.

There are few persons who will deny that boxing, whatever effect it may have on the mind, is a manly sport requiring strength and courage. So the whole question seems to boil down to this:—It is better to foster those qualities of pluck and self-reliance, which have made us what we *are*, than to dabble sentimentally with humane theories which may tend towards national enervation, and make us what we should certainly not like to *become*.

There is a danger, which has been to some extent exemplified in the football field and in other arenas of athletic enterprise, of a bad type of *professionalism*, damaging true sporting characteristics.

It is unnecessary to go into particulars here, and nothing is further from my desire than to say one word against true professionals, whether they be teachers of the various branches of athletics, or those who have honourably competed in the ring for money prizes of all values, from a ten-pound note to a couple of thousand or more; what does appear to stand in the way of true sport is the injudicious and possibly unfair manipulation of pecuniary considerations.

That the decadence of the popularity of certain games and sports will ultimately be traceable to the prevalence of a bad form of professionalism seems highly probable. Horse-racing gets a bad name. Why? because many of the surroundings

INTRODUCTION.

are undesirable, and horses have been pulled, and the final manipulation of the money has come as a surprise. It is not that anything is wrong with the horses or the sport *per se*, it is the outside element that does the mischief.

What may fairly be termed the undesirable factor has done the same for the prize-ring. Probably the vast majority of the old fights were quite *bonâ fide* affairs; then the blackguard element crept in, and the whole business fell into disfavour, and degenerated to such an extent that public confidence was destroyed.

Even in the present-day glove-fights, it is frequently impossible to say for certain "the best man won." We know that gate-money is a factor, and that private arrangements or even intimidation are factors on occasions, and all this tends to destroy the interest and popularity of such contests. Could we but eliminate these objections, together with certain of the more debasing surroundings, we might yet be able to welcome a genuine and healthy revival of the Ring. It is to be hoped that these lines will not meet the eye of any very severe critic or censor, who will construe my humble defence of a practically defunct pastime into an incitement to a breach of the peace, or will try to run me in as an accessory before the fact!

There has been a good deal of cant and insincere nonsense spread over the whole subject, and the late Lord Palmerston put the matter as it probably appeared to the understandings of nine Englishmen out of ten in his day, and possibly his remarks appeal to an equal percentage at the present moment. Referring to the bystanders at fights, he said—"As far as they are concerned, they may conceive it to be a very harmless pursuit; some persons like what takes place; there may be a difference of opinion, as a matter of taste, whether it is a spectacle one would wish to see, or whether it is calculated to excite disgust. Some people look upon it as an exhibition of manly courage, characteristic of the people of this country. I saw the other day," said his lordship, "a long extract from a French newspaper, describing this fight [1] as a type of the national character for endurance, patience under suffering, of indomitable perseverance in determined effort, and holding it up as a specimen of the manly and admirable qualities of the British race. All that is, of course, entirely a matter of opinion; but really, setting

[1] Sayers *v.* Heenan.

aside the legal technicalities of the case, I do not perceive why any number of persons, say 1000 if you please, who assemble to witness a prize-fight, are in their own persons more guilty of a breach of the peace than an equal number of persons who assemble to witness a balloon ascent. There they stand; there is no breach of the peace; they go to see a sight, and when that sight is over they return, and no injury is done to any one. They only sit and stand on the grass to witness the performance, and as to the danger to those who perform themselves, I imagine the danger to life in the case of those who go up in balloons is certainly greater than that of two combatants who merely hit each other as hard as they can, but inflict no permanent injury upon each other."

But then Lord Palmerston was a thorough Englishman to the backbone, and without doubt secretly entertained a liking for the Ring, and admired the courage and endurance so often shown —he had no sympathy with the sentimentalists who at that time made their shrieks echo through the length and breadth of the land.

As regards the legality of modern boxing matches or glove-fights, we have the recent utterances of the late Mr. Justice Cave on the charge of manslaughter brought against one Joseph Williams, who was said to have caused the death of Michael Kerwin at a boxing contest at the Olympic Club, Birmingham. The deceased was boxing with Williams shortly before his death, but it is not quite certain that he did not die from the effects of disease. Even if his death had been caused by the blows complained of, Mr. Justice Cave pointed out to the Grand Jury that sparring matches with gloves, if fairly conducted under ordinary rules, were not unlawful, and consequently the person delivering the blow could not be convicted of manslaughter. This opinion was given on July 30, 1897, and the Grand Jury ignored the bill against Williams.

CHAPTER II.

POSITION AND STYLE.

ALTHOUGH acrobats can put themselves into perplexing attitudes, and do many tricks with great effect when going through the most puzzling contortions, it may be taken for granted that an easy and natural position is the best for most games and sports. "Good form" must be borne in mind, for in no branch of athletics is this more necessary than it is in boxing, and it is probably easier to slip thoughtlessly into a set of bad habits in this than in other exercises. Bad habits once contracted are very difficult to eradicate, indeed, it has been said that it is possible to contract in a month a host of faults which a year's good work will not remove.

You should take every advantage of your height, be able to advance and retreat with equal facility; always have your hands and arms ready for attack or defence, your head in its normal position, and your eyes fixed on your opponent's eyes; while at the same time taking in the whole man from the crown of his head to the sole of his foot.

As on a former occasion, it is my intention to deal first with the feet, and we will suppose that both the men now to be put into position are boxers who spar in the usual way, with left hands and feet in advance.

Draw two parallel lines on the floor, six feet apart, and a third line joining them at right angles to both (Fig. 1). Next draw the parallel dotted lines through the points of intersection, and at an angle of 30° to the first two lines. Let aa' represent the footprints of one man A, and bb' those of his opponent B, a and b being the left, and a' and b' being the right feet. The right foot in each case should be about eighteen inches to the rear of the left foot, and inclined to the line on which that foot rests at an angle of about 45°, and some six inches to the right hand of that line. It will be seen that a good base is thus formed, and this is a matter of no slight importance, for if the feet are directly in line, *i.e.* one just behind the other, you are standing upon a straight line, and are liable to be knocked over sideways; if, on the other hand, both feet are drawn up level, *i.e.* at an equal distance from the opponent, you stand a chance of being knocked over backwards. So we naturally fall into a middle course, and our base is a triangle

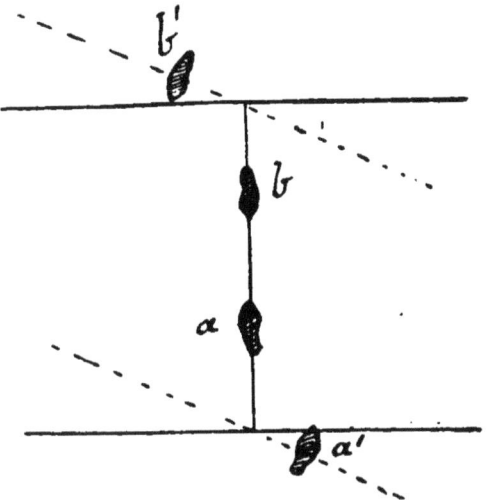

Fig. 1. Position.

formed by lines joining the ball of the left foot to the toe and heel of the right foot. The relative distance of the feet will vary according to the height of the individual.

When standing as just directed, the knees should not be bent, as that only means a diminution of height; neither should they be rigidly stiff, as that means a slight loss of time either in advance or retreat. I have occasionally heard teachers telling their pupils to bend their knees and "sink well down," astounding advice truly, for it means extra fatigue, loss of speed, and a painful and cramped position. Never go in for useless postures the meaning of which cannot be explained. In the following pages it will probably be necessary to allude to what may very properly be called "antics" in boxing; and let me here say once and for all, that an affected style is not only extremely bad form, bringing ridicule upon the exponent, but is prejudicial to really sound work. If an examination of the styles of all the best boxers and fighters, and a careful consideration of mechanical laws lead you to believe in a certain style as *good*, do not allow yourself to be led into copying some tenth-rate man because he happens to have showy tricks, or to have defeated a local pigmy or two. If you do so you will be abandoning the substance for the shadow, and find out the mistake when it is too late.

A point of very vital importance is the direction of the left foot, which should always point directly towards your adversary. If you stand in front of a mirror with the left toe *turned in* and then hit

POSITION AND STYLE.

out towards the glass, you will find that the hit is pulled across, *i.e.* instead of proceeding in a plane at right angles to the mirror it will pursue a slanting direction. If the toe be now pointed straight towards the mirror it will be found that the blow will also be in a straight direction. This point will be enlarged upon in another chapter; here, however, as we are on the subject of position, it is necessary to mention it as being of great importance.

Boxers of great merit have been at variance as to whether it is well to stand very square when facing your man, or very slanting. It seems to me that the inclination should be about the same as that indicated by the dotted lines in Fig. 1, p. 27. The shoulders should be well over the hips, not pushed forward in the hope of getting nearer the opponent, nor thrown back so as to advance the chest and stomach, and thereby court disaster.

The head also should be in its natural position, and no attempt should be made to alter this whilst you are simply standing in position.

Every muscle in the body should be relaxed and easy, anything approaching rigidity tending towards fatigue and slowness. The weight should be evenly divided between the feet, the reasons being that advance and retreat are thus made easier. If you stand, say, with three-quarters of your entire weight on the left, or advanced foot, and want to retreat, it will take longer to shift that weight than it would if you only had half the weight on the left foot. Similarly, with regard to the right foot, if you have three-quarters of your weight on it you will be longer in advancing than you would if properly balanced. That this point is of great importance will be realized when we consider the value of every fraction of a second.

A cramped style is an abomination, and it is therefore evident that every boy should be put into position as early as possible; for he will thus fall into the correct style, which, as time goes on, will become a sort of second nature to him, and there will be less of that painfully strained *effort* to preserve good form. Most animals swim by nature, but an untaught child will probably drown if thrown into deep water; so the motions of swimming, as best adapted to the human frame, are *taught*, and in time become almost second nature. A good style in boxing is evidently not instinctive, seeing that so few people acquire it to anything approaching perfection, and it is well to inculcate sound principles as regards position and all movements from a very early age, before the bones have become set and the muscles consolidated.

If the above remarks on freedom of action in leg work are important, so also are those upon the position and movements of the arms. For men standing as described above, the left arm should work easily and freely in a plane at right angles to the ground, and as nearly as possible following the direction of the left leg and foot. The hand and fore-arm should be regarded *as one piece*, all motion being imparted through the shoulder and elbow joints, which cannot be too free and loose except at the moment of delivering the hit. *The wrist, fore-arm, and back of the hand should be in the same straight line*, otherwise it will be found impossible to deliver an effective blow with the true knuckles, and if the hit gets home, a sprained or fractured wrist may result. All tricky wriggles or "flappy" movements of the hands are to be avoided.

The right hand and fore-arm should *lightly cover the mark, the arm itself being in contact with the body*, and slightly inclining upward towards the left breast. By this means you have *always* an effective guard for the body, and are ready to guard the head by a slight raising of the right hand. Bear in mind here that boxing-gloves must not be looked upon as guards, they are only accessories enabling you to practise fighting without disfigurement. All guards will be made with the arms themselves, as though boxing-gloves were absent.

Do not ever allow either of your hands to drop below the belt, for remember the lower down they get the further they have to travel to reach your opponent or defend yourself.

The elbows should never be stuck out in the "akimbo" style, but should work close to the body, for this is necessary if you want to hit straight. Modifications are always necessary in matters like this. For instance, if you are opposed to a much taller man your hands and arms will be held higher; if your adversary is shorter you will do well to be altogether more "pulled together," so to speak, not only for attack but defence; for the shorter man will go for in-fighting, and endeavour to visit your body with short-arm hits, so that if your arms are near your sides they will form guards to his body blows.

Good boxers are somewhat divided as to the

POSITION AND STYLE.

best method of moving the left hand when not engaged in hitting or guarding. I have seen excellent exponents who go in for hardly moving this hand when not hitting, while others again are to be found who move it very extensively. My own idea is that a slight circular motion in a plane about at right angles to the ground is the soundest plan, for it is less fatiguing than keeping the hand at rest, and certainly not so trying as the vigorous piston-like action adopted by some men.

Slight modifications are often extremely desirable, only be sure that you are working on sound principles, capable of explanation and support in the first instance.

Do not forget to regard your fist and fore-arm as practically a solid piece, and never on any account (except when feinting) show your hit: that is to say, you should be *ever ready to hit out from any position on the imaginary circle in which your hand is moving, without giving your adversary any hint by drawing back the hand preparatory to hitting.* Too much attention cannot be paid to this remark.

It would be profitable to give illustrations of the styles of various boxers from the time of Mendoza, but space will not admit of this, and readers are referred to *Pugilistica*, in the three volumes of which will be found descriptions of the British champions from 1719, when James Fig held his own with the cudgel and back-sword as well as with the fists, up to the time when King and Heenan fought their celebrated battle in 1863.

All the old heroes, Jack Broughton, Dan Mendoza, Humphries, "the Gentleman Boxer," Belcher, Tom Cribb, Tom Spring, Jem Ward, Thompson, "Bendigo," Caunt, Harry Broome, Harry Orme, Tom Paddock, William Perry, "the Tipton Slasher," right up to the later lights of the old prize-ring, King, Sayers, and Mace, may be read of with interest and instruction.

One can imagine the crafty Mendoza, probably most incorrectly described as "one of the most elegant and scientific boxers recorded in the annals of pugilism," standing in the unsatisfactory position he is represented as taking up in his third fight with Humphries; and we can also see how unfavourably his "shaping up" compares with the better exponents of later schools. He is giving away four or five inches of his already short stature; his elbows are akimbo, and he looks thoroughly prepared to deliver short, snatchy hits with either hand, or even the chopping blow from the elbow; in fact, as viewed from our standpoint in the present day, both he and his opponent look like a couple of rustics in for a "bashing" match.

Mendoza beat Humphries in the last and deciding fight, which took place on September 29, 1790, and he appears to have then proved conclusively that he was the better man.

The position and style of Mendoza was probably the best to be had *in those days*, and the exponent himself was evidently a man of strength, experience, and courage, who managed to hold his own wonderfully well, till one day he was unmercifully scragged by Mr. John Jackson, who mauled him severely in a short fight which lasted but little over ten minutes.

Such a style as that obtaining in the days of Mendoza cannot be advocated for a moment, the only wonder is that any man giving away so much in the matter of reach and stability of position ever did any good at all with larger men. It seems probable that Humphries or Mendoza would not be "in it" with the better class of modern fighters.

CHAPTER III.

LEG WORK.

CORRECT methods of standing and getting about the ring are so essential that, before going into the question of hitting and guarding, a few remarks on leg work generally will not be out of place here. All advancing and retreating should be executed as rapidly and silently as possible, and without any stamping, jumping, or excitement. Occasionally it may be necessary to jump back to avoid punishment, or when hopelessly cornered; but as a rule *both feet should not be off the ground at the same time.* A good solid foundation for the feet, with the weight evenly balanced, will greatly assist in carrying this out.

When advancing, step out for the required distance directly towards your opponent with the left, and follow it up with the right foot, so that both feet are in the same relative position as when you started to advance.

Retreating is effected in a similar manner, only the right is withdrawn first and followed up with the left foot, which should still be pointed in the direction of the adversary. These movements should be constantly repeated, and it is not a bad plan to go through them both with long and short steps before or after your morning tub, and in front of a looking-glass, as you will then be able to see at a glance where you are going wrong. By constant practice you will gradually develop a neat and effective advance and retreat. Nothing looks worse or is more prejudicial than a scrambling, shifty, or uncertain method of moving the legs.

At the commencement and end of all such movements the weight should be as nearly as possible evenly balanced on both feet.

One reason why heavy weights are so seldom good all round is that they are not, as a rule, nimble on their pins. Probably more really depends on the legs than on the hands, and my opinion is, that in the early days of the Ring this question was not sufficiently studied. This is why skipping and other spring-encouraging work is so much to be commended, and the reader is here referred to that portion of the book which deals with training and exercises.

In most cases the legs hold out after the wind has gone and the arms and upper portions of the body are exhausted. Still, as all the resources have to be husbanded in any severe contest, it is well to bear in mind that no unnecessary running about should be done. A man who stamps violently about the ring in the vain hope of inspiring terror or distracting his adversary does not advance his own cause in the least, whereas the stealthy, cat-like movements of the expert all mean business, and do not exhaust or jar the limbs.

Probably Peter Jackson, the coloured champion, is as good a man to watch as there is to be found anywhere, and, amongst the retired professionals, Ned Donnelly is very noticeable for the excellency of his leg work.

No doubt the best leg work is to be found amongst the light and middle weights, and possibly one reason for this is, that they are compelled to get about more in order to avoid the punishment of heavier opponents; it is partly a matter of necessity with them—"*necessitas non habet legem*," and partly due to the fact that, being lighter, they are also, as a rule, quicker.

Many a big man has lost a fight through exhausting himself in his efforts to follow a small opponent round a big ring, so don't *over-do* the leg work, which is after all but a means to an end, and more required by middle than heavy, and by light than middle weights.

By all means avoid over-reaching, or getting into a position with your legs from which it is difficult to recover at once. If in a tight place "slipping" and the "side step," of which more anon, may be resorted to with great effect; for very frequently the best guard is found in a short retreat, which as often as not opens up a more effective return than a mere guard with either of the arms would do. As an example of this sort of thing one may mention the side step to right with simultaneous duck and body blow with the left. The above advice seems especially applicable when boxing with a man whose length of reach and general capabilities you have not quite had time to gauge.

Leg work, especially the side step and slipping, is analogous to ducking and stooping to avoid blows, but in making use of these passive defences you should always keep your eye open for the attack which may be opened up to you, *i. e.* don't be satisfied with merely avoiding punishment—

endeavour to make the very avoidance lead up to some hostile movement.

A great deal, of course, depends upon the size of the ring or other place in which you may be boxing or fighting; but rely upon it, the smaller the area to which you are restricted the more perfect should be your leg work, because the more curtailed the space the more the danger of bad results from a mistake such as over-reaching or tripping up.

In a street fight the value of good leg work cannot be over-estimated, for if your legs are well under you, instead of sprawling about all over the place, you are far less liable to a fall, through tripping over a curbstone or other inequality, and *one leg is always ready to help the other at the shortest notice.*

The necessity for good leg work when opposed to heavy metal is remarkably well illustrated in the following account of Tom Sayers' defeat of William Perry, nicknamed "the Tipton Slasher." Sayers was but 5ft. 8½in., and weighed under 11st., whilst the Slasher was over 6ft., and weighed about 14st. 6lbs. It was in this fight that Tom Sayers, the champion middle weight, topped all his previous achievements by wresting the

GETTING OUT OF REACH.

championship of England from the redoubtable holder of the belt. The fight took place on June 16, 1857, and excited, as may be supposed, no little interest in the pugilistic world, some holding that Sayers would not be able to properly reach his man, others again, mindful of his doings with other big 'uns, believing that his superior leg work and general tactics would carry him through to victory.

TOM SAYERS v. "TIPTON SLASHER."

"*Round* 1. On toeing the scratch the contrast between the men was, as may be imagined, most extraordinary. The ould Tipton topped his adversary at least four inches, and it looked, to the uninitiated, 'a horse to a hen.' His immense frame, and ponderous, muscular arms and legs seemed calculated to bear him to victory against four such men as Sayers. He looked all full of confidence, and evidently considered he had a very easy little job before him. He was thinner than we expected to see him, and his condition generally was very fair, but there were the usual indications of age upon certain points where the fulness and roundness of youth had disappeared from his form.

He looked all his age (thirty-eight); indeed by many he was thought to be far on the shady side of forty. His attitude was ungainly, but still he was rough and ready, and the question that suggested itself was, 'How was Sayers to get at him?' Tom Sayers, as he advanced to meet his antagonist, was the perfection of manly strength and athletic development. His fine broad shoulders, small loins, and powerful arms and legs were all turned in one of Nature's best lathes, and there was not a fault to find, unless it was found that he had two or three pounds more flesh than was necessary about his back and ribs. His attitude for attack or defence was admirable, and however confident the Slasher was, it was perfectly obvious that Sayers was not a whit behind in that respect. The Slasher had evidently made up his mind to set to work at once and cut his man down in a jiffy. He lumbered in like a huge bear, let go both hands with more vigour than judgment, but did not get home, and Sayers, in stepping back, fell, but at once jumped up to renew the round. The Slasher went at him, put in a little one on the skull, and Tom again fell.

2. The Slasher came up evidently with greater confidence than ever, and lunged out his right,

which reached Tom's ribs with great force, and Tom countered him sharply on the mouth, drawing 'first blood.' The Slasher looked astonished, stopped to consider a moment, and again went in, swinging his great arms like the sails of a windmill. Sayers danced lightly out of harm's way, and then, stepping in, popped a tidy smack on the spectacle-beam, and got away laughing. After dancing round his man, and easily avoiding several more lunges, Tom again got home on the snuffer-tray, removing a piece of the japan, and drawing a fresh supply of ruby. The Tipton, annoyed, rushed in, missed his right, and also a terrific upper-cut with his left, and Sayers again dropped in upon the nose. After this, slight exchanges took place, the Slasher too slow to be effective. He now chased Sayers all over the ring, the latter dancing round him like a wild Indian, or fleeing like a deer, to draw him after him. The vicious blows aimed by the Slasher all fell upon the air, and his exertions to catch his nimble antagonist caused him to blow off steam to an indefinite extent. Had one of the intended compliments alighted upon Tom, it looked as if it would have been all over with him. After Sayers had completed his dance he went to his man, cleverly avoided a good right-hander, and delivered another very hot one on the proboscis (more 'Lafitte' of the premier *crû*). The Tipton tried his heavy punches again three times and missed; a fourth attempt was prettily stopped, after which both hit short. The Tipton next got on Tom's right cheek with his left, but not heavily, and some very pretty stopping followed on both sides, after which the Tipton made another rush like a bull at a gate, and found himself once more battling with vacancy, Tom having slipped under his arm, and danced off laughing. The Slasher looked with astonishment, and shook his nut. Sayers again approached, and after one or two feints a good exchange took place, Sayers getting on to the left eye, and the Slasher on the ribs. Sharp counter hits followed, Slasher on the mouth and Tom on the cheek. Tom now led off with his double, but the Slasher stopped him prettily twice in succession, when he missed his return. The Slasher again pounded away, principally with his right, but without effect, as Sayers jumped back or stopped every effort. Sayers now planted a stinger with his left on the mark and stopped the return. The next minute he got sharply home on the nasal organ, and jumped quickly away from a well-intended upper-cut, which looked like a finisher. The Slasher now stopped one or two pretty leads, but his return came so slowly that Sayers was far out of harm's way. This occurred several times, the Slasher rushing about like a baited bull, Sayers skipping and nimbly getting away from every rush. After a little of this entertainment Sayers went in, let go his left, and was stopped neatly, and he, in turn, stopped two very round hits on the part of Perry. Sayers next feinted, and got home a slashing left-hander on the right cheek, which he cut severely, and drew a plenteous supply of ruby. Another hit fell on the same spot. The Slasher then got a little one on Tom's body, and tried again, but Tom got away. The Slasher retired to his corner to get his mug wiped, and on coming out again, Tom led him another dance all over the ring, the old one, with more haste than speed, trying to catch him, and repeatedly expending his strength in empty space. At last Sayers, having given him a good turn at this game, stopped to see whether he was pumped, and some good exchanges followed, Sayers again on the damaged cheek, and the Slasher also reaching the cheek. Mutual stopping followed, and Sayers next got home heavily on the olfactory projection. The Slasher now stopped

Tom, and returned, but not heavily, on the top of his nut, which led to exchanges, Tom on the left optic and Bill on the ribs. After one or two more exchanges, another tremendous counter took place, Tom receiving on the mouth, and the Slasher on the nose, each drawing the carmine. The Slasher having next made several misses went in, and another sharp encounter was exchanged, Tom receiving on the brain-pan, and the Slasher on the beak, from which more home-brewed escaped. Each now had a wipe of the sponge, and Tom treated his opponent to another game of follow-my-leader all over the ring, in the course of which the Slasher caught him a heavy right-hander on the back. He then stopped Tom's left and heavy encounters followed, Tom on the nose and the Slasher on the *os frontis*, knocking him down (first 'knock-down' for Slasher). This round lasted nearly half-an-hour.

3. The Slasher came up laughing, but he was evidently bent on mischief. Sayers smiled, tried his left, and was stopped, and the Slasher, as usual, missed two swinging right-handers. Tom dodged, popped his left on the mark, and then on the forehead, got a little one on the ribs, and exchanges followed, Tom getting home on the

left ogle, and Tipton on the mouth. Some heavy give-and-take fighting followed, Tom getting more juice from the Slasher's right cheek, and receiving one or two smart ones on the neck and side of his head. Mutual stopping, feinting, and dodging until Tom got home on the mark, and the Slasher again followed him all over the ring, hitting out of distance, and with no manner of judgment. Finding he could do nothing, the Slasher put down his hands and retired for another wipe from Jack Macdonald, and then renewed his exertions, when some pretty stopping took place on both sides, after which Sayers got home on the left side of the nob, but was stopped in another essay. The Slasher stopped two more well-intended ones, and then got home on the side of Tom's cranium; Sayers returned now heavily on the proboscis, once more turning on the tap. Tom now dodged, and then got home heavily on the damaged cheek—a tremendous hit, and again did the home-brewed appear. The Slasher retired to be cleaned, and came again viciously, but Sayers pinked him on the smeller, receiving a slight return on the top of the nob. More futile efforts on the part of the Slasher, whose friends called upon Sayers to stand still and be hit, but Tom wisely declined. He had orders to keep his man on his legs and fight him at long shots, and these orders he carried out most excellently. Again and again did the Slasher miss or get stopped. Occasionally he got home a very little one, which did not leave a mark, and now he rushed at Tom, dashed out his right, and very narrowly escaped smashing his fist against the stake—it was within an inch. Sayers lifted up his arms with astonishment and stood laughing, until the Slasher wore round on another tack, and came at him again, when Tom got away, shaking his noddle and grinning. The Slasher followed, Tom nailed him on the nozzle, stopped his return, and then planted another on the cheek. Sharp exchanges followed, the Slasher getting on Tom's right cheek and just drawing the juice, while Tom left a mark on the Slasher's left eye. The old 'un, very slow, sparred apparently for wind, and was then stopped left and right, after which each hit over the shoulder. Tom afterwards stopped both hands, and got easily away from a third attempt. Slight exchanges followed, Tom on the nose, and Slasher on the top of the head. More dancing by Sayers, and exhausting efforts on the part of the Slasher; and then as the Slasher came, Tom caught him a severe straightener on the snuff-box, drawing lots of claret. The Slasher, savage, stood to consider, and then rushing in delivered a little one on the side of Tom's head with his right, and Tom fell. (Time, fifty-two minutes.)

4. The Slasher came up grinning, but he was evidently somewhat fatigued by his exertions. He nevertheless adhered to his practice of forcing the fighting, and again dashed at Tom, and contrived to plant a little one on the body with his right, but it was not within punishing distance. Slight exchanges followed on the side of the wig-block, after which the Slasher stopped Tom's left. Heavy counter-hits next succeeded in favour of Sayers, who got home on the Slasher's potato-trap, and napped a little one on the nob. After another dance round the ring Tom stopped the Slasher's right, and the latter then drove him into the corner, and evidently thinking he had him safe, wound himself up to finish; but when he let go his left and right, he found that Tom had slipped under his arm, and was laughing at him in the middle of the ring. The K-legged giant, irate that his opponent would not stand to be hit, again lumbered after him, like an elephant in pumps, but it was no go. 'No catchee, no havee' was Tom's

maxim, and he kept to his active tactics. The Slasher persevered, and Sayers stopped his left and right, and then turned away laughing and shaking his noddle. The Tipton giant could not make it out, and turned to his second as if to inquire what he should do; another illustration of the classical adage—*capit consilium gladiator in arena.* At last he went at it again and got home on the body, receiving in return on the kisser. Some sparring followed, until the Tipton again led off, and was short with both hands. Finding he could do nothing, he retired to his corner, where he stood leaning on the ropes, Tom waiting and beckoning him to the scratch. After a rest the Slasher came out, feinted at Tom, but was quickly nailed on the left cheek. He tried again, and got home heavily on the ribs, and Sayers fell. (Time, one hour and four minutes.)

5. Perry still adhered to his boring tactics, but Tom was far too quick on his pins, and easily avoided him. Another attempt was stopped, and from a third Sayers got easily away. A fourth was missed, and Tom returned on the left cheek, which led to heavy exchanges on the side of the head, and Tom fell, the Slasher falling over him.

6. The Slasher came up laughing, and let go his left, but out of distance; good exchanges followed, Sayers effecting another lodgment on the right cheek, and increasing the cut in that quarter, and the Slasher getting home on the cranium. The Slasher, after another ill-directed rush, again retired to his corner, had a drink and a wipe, and then came again, when Sayers stopped his deliveries with the greatest ease. The Slasher persevered, and Tom led him another morris-dance, but they afterwards got close, and slight exchanges ended in the Slasher falling.

7. The Tipton bored in stooping, head foremost, like a bull of Salamanca. Tom not being provided with a mantilla to throw over his head jumped aside like a matador, and on went his assailant to the ropes. Perry swung round, just got on to Tom's head, and each then missed a blow. The Slasher persevered, and Tom countered on the left side of his forehead with his right, after which Perry retired to his corner, whither Sayers followed him, and the Slasher at once lunged out at the cheek, but not effectually. He now made another of his wild onslaughts, but only to be disappointed, and he next stopped both Tom's mauleys. Some sparring followed, both being slightly blown; the

Slasher stopped Tom's left, and returned with his right on the body. After a few more misses they got close, and Tom delivered a heavy spank on the left eye, and fell from the force of his own blow. (One hour and fifteen minutes.)

8. Perry showed a bump under the left peeper, but he came up smiling, and let go his left and right, both of which were stopped. He then stood blowing, until Sayers went to the attack, and some mutual pretty stopping took place, followed by several misses on either side. The Slasher once more retired to rest in his corner, but was fetched out by Sayers, who then got home on the side of the nob, and neatly avoided a return. Both were now rather wild in their lunges, and the Slasher, who pursued his man most vigorously, repeatedly missed his blows. Tom at length caught him on the cut-water, drawing a fresh supply from the beet-bin, and the Slasher walked off to borrow Jack Macdonald's wipe. Tom followed, and got home very heavily on the mark and then on the mouth, renewing 'the cataract from the cavern.' Sharp exchanges in favour of Sayers followed, and in the end both fell.

9. The Slasher came up slowly. Notwithstanding his severe punishment, his seconds sent

LEG WORK.

him up beautifully clean, and in fact their attention throughout was beyond all praise. He tried again and again to plant upon the agile Sayers, but in vain. Sayers stopped him at all points, and then delivered a heavy left-hander on the mark. Some sparring followed, and Sayers stopped several heavy lunges, the Tipton in return stopping his left. Tom in another attempt got on the damaged cheek, increasing the cut, and the Tipton walked to his corner, whither Tom followed him, but on the Slasher making his usual lunge Sayers jumped back. Perry followed, and some pretty taps and stops, without mischief, took place. The Slasher then hit out of distance several times in succession, but on getting close some neat exchanges followed, Tom on the mark, heavily, and Perry on the cheek, but not effectively. Perry once more bored in and delivered his right, but it was a mere fly-blow. Tom missed his prop with the left, and the Slasher retired for a drink. Tom thought this an example worth following, and after the inner man was refreshed, they went to work again, and sharp exchanges, all in favour of Sayers, followed; he kept playing on the Slasher's damaged nose and cheek, his double being very effective, while Perry's blows appeared to leave no mark. Tom now stopped several well-intended blows, and returned heavily on the right cheek with his left. Perry, although getting slower every minute, gamely persevered, put in his right and left on the body, and then hit short with both hands. More mutual stopping ensued, until they got close, when the Slasher dashed his right at the body, but Tom met him with a very straight left-hander on the mouth, drawing more of the elixir of life, and with his right he planted severely on the nose. Another sharp one on the mouth caused the Slasher to stagger and fall, and Tom fell over him. The Slasher evidently was fast going; the last three blows, particularly the right-hander, were very heavy, and the game old fellow was almost abroad, and was very slow to time.

10 and last. The Slasher crawled very slowly to the scratch, and attempted to lead off. It was, however, only an attempt. Tom easily avoided it, and planted a tremendous hit on the mark, stopping the return with ease. He stopped two more attempts, and then as the Slasher lunged out a third time, he caught him with the left on the damaged cheek, and the right on the mouth, cutting his upper lip very severely, and the Slasher fell, Tom on him. The Slasher was carried to his

LEG WORK.

corner, and, with some difficulty, was got round in time to go to the scratch for another round. His dial, however, was dreadfully punished, and his lip was so much cut that he presented a piteous appearance. It was evident that he had not the slightest chance; he was as weak as a kitten, and entirely at the mercy of his adversary, who was perfectly scatheless, and apparently as active as when he began; and Owen Swift, the Slasher's principal backer, seeing the state of things, stepped into the ring, and with praiseworthy humanity declared that he should fight no more. Perry was very unwilling to give up without one more shy, but Owen was imperative. He insisted upon the men shaking hands, and the sponge was thrown up, Tom Sayers being proclaimed the winner, and Champion of England, amid the cheers of his partisans, at the expiration of one hour and forty-two minutes."

Though Sayers did so well, there is no doubt that he really overdid it in the leg work, and exerted himself quite unnecessarily. It would have been sheer folly for him to stand up and court give and take and exchanges with a man of the Slasher's immense weight and strength. He played the 'game throughout to the satisfaction of his backers—avoiding punishment, and popping in his hits whenever an opening was presented. He merely erred on the side of caution, and displayed a quite unnecessary amount of agility: had Perry been more active this waste of energy might have told against him severely in the finish. No better example of leg work, somewhat carried to excess, could be found in the annals of the Ring than was afforded in the above-quoted fight.

LEAD OFF WITH THE LEFT—TOE STRAIGHT. CORRECT; HIT STRAIGHT.

CHAPTER IV.

ON STRAIGHT HITTING.

ONE sometimes reads of a fight in which the winner has vanquished his man by using swinging circular hits, but it is important not to be misled by the apparent significance of the result; for it simply means that success has been achieved through good fortune, superior strength, endurance or training.

Never lose sight of the fact that *there is no nearer way between any two points than a straight line.* The points in this case are your hand and some part of your opponent's anatomy, and there is no quicker line of route than the straight line lying between them. In my opinion there is only one case in which this should be deviated from, and that is when the half-arm or contracted-arm hit is made use of at close quarters, or in the delivery of the upper cut, of which mention will be made in a future chapter.

All natural fighters hit round, and it is to get over this tendency, so strongly marked in the tyro, that good teachers keep their pupils for such long periods at practising straight leads with the left.

Watch two men who know nothing of boxing, and note carefully the number of occasions on which they completely miss their mark through taking swinging hits at one another, and now let us inquire into the reason of this.

Supposing A is the position of one man's head

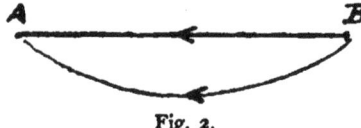

Fig. 2.

and B the position of the other's hand. There are four points which will at once occur to the reader.

1. The distance by the straight line from B to A is shorter than that by the curve, and therefore, *cæteris paribus*, time will be saved.

2. It is harder to calculate the time at which the swinging hit will arrive, and a slight advance or retreat on the part of your adversary will cause you to miss him altogether.

3. By adopting this swing round you are very apt to expose yourself, for you will probably no

longer face your man, but will present a side opening to him, and this is not the case if the blow be straight.

4. Recovery is not so rapid.

We must not be oblivious of the fact that many dangerous hits may be delivered in this faulty style by a powerful opponent, and they should be carefully watched. The best defence is a slight retreat— only just sufficient to get out of the way—and an immediate return. Or, say he swings at you with the left, you may often duck to the right and land your own left heavily on his face or body, since he swings well on to your blow and meets it.

Later on it will be necessary to go into the question of round hitting more fully; in the present chapter we are dealing with the best means of acquiring the art of really hitting straight.

A loose and free style of taking up position has previously been alluded to as of importance, and the reason for this will become evident directly you begin to practise your leads. It always takes an appreciable time to get a stiff, muscle-bound man to move at all: there is a strained rigidity which has to be dispelled before the hit has even started, and *this initial loss of time can never be recovered.*

Speed is everything, and, though there are

degrees in this as in other qualities, and practice will generally develop improvement, it is hard to expect much unless the muscles and tendons are flexible and free in their action. Therefore give yourself every chance by standing in an easy attitude with all the joints loose and mobile.

If, then, you are standing as indicated in a previous chapter, and wish to lead off at your adversary's head, slightly raise the left foot and advance it along the line for a couple of feet, simultaneously hitting out straight at the enemy's head. In doing this remember that *there must be no previous indication of the movement either by shuffling the feet or drawing back the hand and so showing the hit.* The body should be well thrown forward at the same time with a good spring from the right foot, which should not, however, leave the ground. Be careful not to over-reach yourself, and let the *weight of the body fully enter into the hit.*

The hand should reach its destination shortly before the left foot touches the ground in the forward step, *at the moment of impact the fist should be tightly clenched*, and the joints of the wrist, elbow, and shoulder should then, and then only for the moment, be rigid and fully extended.

LEAD OFF WITH THE LEFT—TOE TURNED IN. INCORRECT; HIT PULLED ACROSS.

ON STRAIGHT HITTING.

Having executed this manœuvre, the next thing is to instantly recover and return to the position from which you started. Practice only, and that careful practice which the importance of the matter deserves, will enable you to do this gracefully and with very little effort. The above remarks about over-reaching are to be carefully borne in mind, since the recovery is bound to be unsteady if the forward lunge has been at all overdone. At the same time, do not in avoiding Scylla run on to the rocks of Charybdis. If it is bad to over-extend yourself, it is, if anything, worse to develop a short, snatchy style of hitting.

Always let your hit *really be a hit*, and let it go well and freely out like the piston-rod of an engine. When delivering the hit we are considering *make full use of the width of your shoulder*, for if this is not done many inches of the "reach" are lost and the hit is not so powerful, as will be seen from the following considerations.

It is believed that every mechanical power known to science has its exemplar in some portion of the human frame; and certain it is that by changing the configuration or disposition of our limbs and bodies we materially alter their effective power, though we are quite unable to add to or detract from the amount of that power in the system at any given moment.

An examination of the illustration (Fig. 2) will show that there must be a line of resistance, more or less in the form of an arc or bow, running from the point of impact in the left-hand knuckles down the left arm, through the body, and down the right leg to the foot. Now the more this line lies in one plane the greater will be the mechanical advantage; if, therefore, the left shoulder is thoroughly well advanced, we shall, approximately of course, have all our force acting in one plane. Suppose, however, that the shoulder is not thus advanced, the line above-mentioned will not lie in the same plane, and there cannot be the same mechanical advantage, since what is technically termed a "couple" will be found, or, in plainer language, the shoulder will be more easily twisted through not having the power *directly behind it.*

The illustration on p. 198 will, it is hoped, give some idea of how to lead off with the left, and it is almost impossible, when we run our eyes down the long vista of fights snatched from the fire by a good steady straight left, to put too much emphasis on the necessity of practising it more than any of the other hits. We have not indeed

ON STRAIGHT HITTING. 63

to look far for an additional and most cogent reason for giving it most of our attention. It may be regarded as purely scientific and altogether *acquired*, for no one was ever born who started hitting straight by the light of Nature.

The art of putting in this hit with great rapidity, with all the weight of the body along with it, and perfectly straight, is only understood by the few. One may "aim at perfection, but can only achieve improvement," and the truth of this comes home painfully in the early days of learning to really lead off with the left. It has been suggested that practice before a looking-glass on every available occasion is an excellent plan for keeping a man up to the mark, for one is able to notice the effect of mistakes, and especially of the way in which any turning in of the left toe tends to pull the hit across.

Some people advocate hitting at a captive football suspended from the roof, but it is better to get an opponent whose good and bad points you should carefully note. When sparring free always think out everything, and try to answer your mental queries to yourself with *reasons*. This will help to put you on the road to fight with your brains as well as with your arms and legs. Watch everything you see. "Why does that tall man hit so short?" Because he does not make any use of the width of his shoulder. "Why cannot young —— hit a print in a pat of butter?" Because he fails to put the weight of his body into his hits. "Why is Jones so often getting punished—he seems strong?" Because he is as rigid as a Burmese idol, and will never make a boxer. It is by making inquiries of this kind that your mind at last begins to dwell upon and absorb the subject, and even in sleep you may think out the reasons for much you have seen in the daytime.

Sometimes, when you have led off and the adversary has got out of distance without a return, you may advance the right foot and make a second or third hit, and this often stops a man who may think you are about to retreat, and may be bent on following you up.

The best general position for the hand is half-turned with the true or hitting knuckles and back of the hand slanting towards the ground. Modifications are necessary, as, for example, in the cross-counters and body blows, but in leads with the left the above will be found about correct.

Avoid what is called "chopping," *i.e.* hitting down on to your opponent's guard. It is a bad fault, and one most natural and easily acquired. In almost every other form of hitting we do hit down, from hammering in a tintack to emphasizing our remarks in the pulpit or on the platform. The chopping hit too has the disadvantage of being less effective than a box on the ear, and is to be discouraged as a type of round hitting.

Find out by experiment exactly the length of your reach when you are properly extended, and making full use of—

1. Your forward step.
2. Your length of arm.
3. Your width of shoulder.

This will be of assistance; but as you go on you will, if your eye be good, soon get into the way of judging distances to a nicety.

As few fights were of a more determined character or gave better illustration of the value of a good left hand, this has seemed an appropriate place for an account of the battle between Tom Sayers and Nat Langham, and to follow this up with a description of the more famous draw between Sayers and Heenan.

LANGHAM v. SAYERS.

This fight took place near Lakenheath, in Sussex, on October 18, 1853, and is thus given in *Pugilistica*—

"*Round* 1. On toeing the scratch, the knowing ones eagerly scanned the appearance and condition of the men, in order, if possible, to gain thus some indication of the possible issue of the combat, and a few bets were made at 6 to 4 on Langham. There was a wide contrast between the men, both in appearance and condition; Langham was long and lathy; his frame was evidently that of a man who had seen severe work, and—to all appearance—not likely to last through the wear and tear of long-continued exertion. There was a smile of good-humoured confidence on his mug, however, that showed how little he feared the result of the coming combat, while his condition was simply perfect, and reflected the highest credit on his trainer. Sayers, on the other hand, although he looked—as of old—broad, strong, and burly, was clearly overburdened with flesh—the 5lbs. he scaled above his accustomed 10st. 7lbs. being palpably all to the bad. The breaking out on his chin and face certainly did not give one the idea of his being in a perfect state of health, and it may well be that to the fact of his not being in his best form, may be attributed an anxious look about his eyes, so different to the gay, laughing confidence he exhibited in his other fights. Both men, on taking up position, stood with their legs too wide apart; their guards were neither easy nor graceful, nor was there anything strikingly artistic in their attitudes. They began with a good deal of sparring, and at length Langham let go his left, but did not get quite home. Caution was again the order of the day, until Langham once more got within distance, and tried his left a second time, just reaching Tom's chest. Sayers now tried to draw his man, but Langham was not to be had; Sayers, therefore, approached him, when Langham popped in his left on the cheek, and then the same hand on the nose, and got away. Sayers soon followed him up, and Nat, as he retreated, again sent out his left on the cheek. More sparring now took place, and at length counter-hits were exchanged, Nat catching Tom on the chin and drawing first blood from a pimple below his mouth. Sayers now bored in, and caught Nat a nasty one on the forehead, from the effects of which Langham went to grass. (First knock-down blow for Sayers.) Little merit, however, could be attached to it, as the ground was in such a state from the previous day's rain as to render it difficult for Nat to keep his legs, and the hit rather helped him to grass than fairly sent him there. Having now had an opportunity of judging and comparing the men, the betting settled down to 5 to 4 on Nat, the odds being principally due to Tom's obviously bad condition, and to the fact that, having lost the toss for choice of corners, he had to fight with the sun in his eyes.

2. In this round Nat commenced the saving game, which he persisted in throughout the fight, and after planting a tap on the mouth, and receiving on the forehead, slipped down.

3. Both men ready to the call of time, and Langham led off, but the blow fell short on Tom's chest. A second attempt was more successful, as he got home a heavy spank on Tom's snout, from which the ruby was instantly visible. Left-handed counter-hits followed, each getting it slightly on the cheek, and Nat in getting back slipped down.

4. On getting within distance both went to work. Tom made his left on Nat's cheek, and

his right rather heavily on his ribs. Heavy counter-hits followed, in favour of Nat, whose length gave him the advantage. Tom napped in again severely on the smeller, just between the eyes, and returned on Nat's side of his head and his short ribs, the latter a sounding right-hander. Langham now retreated, and, as Tom followed him up, pinked him twice in succession with effect on the nozzle, drawing more claret. Sayers returned slightly on the ribs, and again was met by Nat on the mouth and left eye. Sayers continued to persevere, occasionally getting in a little one on Nat's ribs, but Nat in this round appeared to have it his own way; he propped his man repeatedly on the nose and mouth, and then on the dexter eye. Again and again did Sayers go to it, but Nat jobbed him with it severely on the old spot, and at length finished the round by going down, Sayers walking away his face brightly crimsoned by Nat's handiwork.

5. Nat, on getting his man, let go with his left with great quickness on Tom's nose, completely over his guard. Sayers then went to in-fighting, and got home his left on the side of Nat's knowledge-box, and after a slight rally both went down. A claim of foul was made, that Sayers had hit Nat

while down, but it was not allowed, the man being on the ropes when the blow was delivered.

6. Tom came up grinning, but his mug was in anything but grinning order. Langham, as usual, led off, but Tom jumped away. Tom now feinted, let go his left on Nat's jaw, and then repeated the dose without return. Some rattling exchanges followed in favour of Sayers, and in the end Langham fell.

7. Langham attempted to plant his left, but was out of distance. Two more efforts were frustrated by Tom jumping away. Nat was not to be denied; he went in, and some rattling exchanges took place in favour of Sayers, who got home on Nat's cheek and ribs with severity, and received one or two on the kissing organ, from which more pink was drawn, and Langham in getting back fell.

8. Langham dodged his man, and again popped in his left with great quickness over his guard, turning on the tap. Sayers returned slightly on the cheek, and, on trying to improve upon this, was countered heavily on the mouth. This led to some rapid exchanges in favour of Sayers, who got home heavily on the ribs and jaw, and received on the nasal promontory. The round finished by Langham going to the earth apparently weak.

ON STRAIGHT HITTING.

9. Sayers came up with a visible puffiness under both eyes. Langham, as usual, led off on Tom's mouth. Sayers returned left and right on the canister and ribs, received another little one on the nose, and then lunged out with his right a sounding spank on the side. Langham retreated, and was followed up by Tom, who caught him on the mouth with his left, and Nat, after an ineffectual attempt to return, fell.

10. Langham stepped back to draw his man, who came for it, and again napped an awkward one on the snout. Sayers tried a return, but was short, and got another smack on the nose for his pains. Counter-hits followed, Nat getting it rather heavily on the left eye, and Tom on the nose. Nat, after placing a little one on the nose, fell on his south pole.

11. Langham opened the pleadings by another well-delivered spank on the proboscis, from his left, over Tom's guard. It was wonderful to see how completely Sayers' index seemed to be within reach of Nat's straight-darting deliveries. Left-handed exchanges followed, but Sayers appeared to hit short. Langham delivered again with severity on the bridge of the nose, when Sayers made a one, two (the left on the side of the head,

and his right on the ribs), and Langham got down on the saving suit.

12. A pause now took place, and some mutual feinting and dodging, it being 'bellows to mend' on each side. Nat at length tried his left, which was prettily stopped. Sayers now went in, made his left and right on the nose and ribs, but not heavily. Langham retaliated on the nose, which led to some slight exchanges, and a close, at the end of which both fell, Langham under.

13. Sayers attempted to take the lead, but was propped heavily on the snuff-box. He, however, got in his right with severity on the ribs, and then his left on Nat's cheek. Nat's returns were rendered abortive by the activity of Tom, who again visited his ribs heavily with his right, and Langham fell, Tom falling over him.

14. Langham resumed his lead, and got well on to Tom's damaged nose and mouth—Sayers' nose and cheeks puffing visibly, to the great danger of his clear sight for attack or defence. Tom countered him heavily on the cheek and ribs, and Langham fell, Tom on him.

15. Sayers went to his man, and planted his left on the side of Nat's brain-pan. Langham returned

on the neck with his right, a round hit, and fell in getting away.

16. Nat sent in his left over Tom's guard, upon his nose heavily, and again turned on the main. Good counters followed, Nat on the nose, and Tom on the neck heavily. Exchanges in which Tom got on to Nat's left cheek, and Langham got down, Sayers falling over him.

17. Langham was short in two attempts with his left, and a third was stopped, when Sayers dashed out his left, getting home on the ribs. Langham returned with good effect on the nose, and both fell.

18. Long sparring until Nat let fly his left on the old spot. Tom made his right on the ribs, but again got a nasty crack on the side of his cranium, and Langham got down.

19. Nat was again short in his lead. Tom was more successful, got home his right on the ribs, and Nat was again down.

20. This was a good round on both sides. After a little sparring Langham tried his left, but Tom jumped well away. In a second attempt Nat got slightly home on the chest, and then on the nose. Sayers countered him on the mouth, and then some exchanges took place, in which Nat hit the

straightest, Tom's blows appearing to be open-handed. Sayers now went in, but got it heavily on the nose from Nat, who fought on the retreat. Tom followed him up, got well home on the jaw, and then on the nose and left eye, knocking Langham clean off his legs. (A fair knock-down blow.)

21. The last blow delivered by Sayers was evidently a stinger, as Nat's left peeper and nose showed the effects of it. Tom immediately led off, got in his left and right on the nose and ribs without a return, and then, closing, threw Langham a back-fall, and fell heavily on him. (5 to 4 offered by an enthusiastic backer of Tom's.)

22. Hitting over Tom's guard, Nat got well on Tom's nose, but Sayers returning heavily on the mouth; Nat got back, and fell.

23. Odds of 5 to 4 on Sayers were now freely offered all round the ring, and he certainly seemed to have much the best of it, was full of confidence, and at once opened proceedings by sending in his left heavily on Nat's ivory-box. The latter tried to get away, but Tom followed him up closely, and again landed him on the mouth, avoiding the return. Severe counter-hitting followed, in which Sayers again got on to Nat's mouth, but received

on the smeller, and then Langham went to the earth in a decided state of weakness.

24. Sayers, attempting to force the fighting all he could, again led off on Nat's left cheek, and Nat retaliated on the nose heavily. Tom retreated, and, on going to it again, popped in his right on Nat's commissariat department. He tried a repetition of this, but napped it severely on the nose for his pains. After some sparring Tom reached Nat's ribs, and the latter, reaching his own corner, got down.

25. Sayers, first to begin, delivered a little one on Nat's nose, but the blow wanted steam. Nat retreated, and as Tom followed him, Nat jobbed him on the nozzle, again disturbing the cochineal; and on receiving a little one on the chin Nat dropped.

26. Nat began the attack by a successful endeavour to resume his lead. He got home heavily on Tom's left cheek, which led to exchanges in favour of Nat, who repeatedly met Tom in the middle of the head. Tom got in one or two on the ribs and chest, and one on Nat's left peeper, but not heavily. Nat returned on the face, and in retreating slipped down.

27. Langham again made play on Tom's nose,

the cork being drawn. He got in a little one on the ribs in return, and Nat fell, Sayers on him.

28. On coming up Nat led off, but misjudged his distance and was short, the blow falling on Tom's cheek. Tom sent out his left, but got a very heavy one on his mouth in return. Some heavy exchanges followed, in which Tom got well home on Nat's cheek, from the effect of which Nat fell.

29. One hour had now elapsed, and still there was no decided lead. Langham was again short in his opening deliveries, and Sayers, after returning on the left cheek, closed and threw his man, falling heavily on him.

30. Nat's left once more fell short of its destination, when Tom let out his left and caught him on the mouth; Langham returned quickly on the nose, from which once more the ruby trickled. Slight exchanges followed and Langham fell, evidently weak.

31. Sayers led off, caught Nat a heavy cross hit with his left over the left peeper, inflicting a deep cut and drawing the carmine; he in return had his cork drawn by Nat's left. Some exchanges followed, in the course of which Tom again opened the cut over Nat's left ogle by a heavy hit from his left and Nat fell.

ON STRAIGHT HITTING. 77

32. Another good round. Nat's left peeper looked the worse for wear, but he came gamely up, and as Tom led off he countered him on the nose. Some exchanges followed in favour of Sayers, who got well on Nat's left cheek, and received a return on the cheek-bone. They now got to work in earnest, and some ding-dong fighting took place, as if both thought this the turning-point of the battle. Each got it heavily on the frontispiece, Sayers re-opening the cut over Nat's left eye, and receiving one or two awkward reminders on the cheek and nose. A break away followed, and then Langham again went up to his man, who met him on the left eye another heavy spank. Nat returned on the nozzle, and immediately afterwards received another reminder on the sinister peeper, and fell. This was a capital fighting round, exhibiting the determined resolve of both men.

33. Sayers led off, got home slightly on the throat, and received a heavy one from Nat's left on the right cheek. Excellent counter-hits followed, Tom on the cheek and Nat on the right peeper, and Nat then got down.

34. Long sparring, Langham evidently wanting wind, and Tom not much better. At last Nat

went to work, got well on Tom's damaged nose with his left, and stopped Tom's return. Sayers tried again, and succeeded in reaching Nat's throat, when the latter again fell.

35. Another fighting round. Good counter-hits, each receiving on the left eye. A break away and more counter-hitting, Sayers on the left peeper, and Nat well on the nose. Langham now lunged out his right with great force, but, luckily for Tom, the blow missed its destination, and Nat, over-reaching himself, fell.

36. Nat, on coming up, showed his left peeper in deep mourning, and nearly closed; he was evidently weak, and the friends of Sayers were up in the stirrups. Sayers feinted, and let out his left, which reached the damaged optic, re-opening the former wound. Langham was short in his return. Sayers twice got home his left on the throat, but was stopped in the third attempt; he afterwards succeeded in reaching Nat's left cheek, and the latter, after an ineffectual attempt to return, got down.

37. In spite of the punishment he had received in the previous round, Langham was first up, and he sent out his left, but Tom jumped quickly away, returned heavily on the forehead and ribs, and then fell.

38. Some ineffectual countering, after which Sayers got nearer, and put in a little one on the left eye. Nat retreated, and on being followed by Tom, who delivered straight on the mouth, got down weak.

39. There could be no question as to the gallantry with which both men were fighting, and although appearances were in favour of Sayers, there were not wanting those who saw the danger lying before him, and among these must assuredly be numbered Nat's clever seconds, under whose directions and advice Langham now seemed to devote himself to land just one blow on Tom's swollen nose, or on one of his puffy eyes, and then to get down with as little punishment and as little exertion as possible; for it was impossible to conceal Nat's weakness, and it was decidedly a moot point whether he would be able to hold out until Tom could be forced to 'put up the shutters.' Nat tried to lead off, but was stopped. Sayers attempted to return, but Nat sent out his left very straight on the left eye, and on Sayers again coming on, he delivered the same hand on Tom's damaged smeller, and drew more claret. Tom made his left slightly on the cheek, and Nat at once went to grass.

40. Tom let go his left, got slightly home on the

chest, and Nat, after returning with his left on the forehead, fell.

41. Sayers tried to take the lead, but Nat jumped quickly away; Sayers followed him up, when Nat met him with a sharp tap on the left eye, and then another left-hander on the cheek. Sayers persevered until he got home his right on Nat's ribs, when the latter again got down.

42. Nat led off, caught Tom heavily on the left cheek, and then on the brow. He tried to repeat the visitation, when Tom caught him sharply over the right peeper, drawing blood, and Nat got down. Nat's length and cleverness were conspicuous in his left-hand deliveries.

43. Sayers rushed in, but Nat countered him on the left peeper. Sayers got in his right heavily on the bread-basket, and Nat fell.

44. After a little sparring, the men got close together, and some sharp counter-hits were exchanged, Tom getting well on to Nat's damaged left peeper and receiving on the right cheek. Nat now attempted another delivery, but over-reached himself and fell.

45. The temporary revival of Langham's strength seemed at an end. Sayers let go his left, got home on the cheek, and Nat, who was decidedly

in 'queer street,' again went down sick and weak.

46. Nothing done. Nat got down as soon and as easily as he could manage it.

47. Sayers led off, and caught Nat over the left ogle; this led to some counter-hits, in which Langham got home heavily on Tom's right peeper, which was now pretty nearly closed from the repeated hits on the nose and its exposure to the bright rays of the sun. Langham received a little one on the left cheek in return, and fell.

48. Tom led off, but was countered by Nat on the left eye. In a second attempt Nat stopped him, and then popped him heavily on the nose, drawing more of the ruby. Nat succeeded in planting another heavily on the left peeper, and Tom fell for the first time for many rounds.

49. Things looked by no means so cheerful for Sayers' backers, for although he was by far the stronger man on his pins, he now came up bleeding from both eyes, his seconds having been compelled to lance them while he was in his corner, to prevent his going blind. He dashed in, aware that although much the stronger man on his legs, he must be in total darkness if he did not finish his man soon. Slight exchanges took place, Tom

getting it on both eyes slightly, and returning, but without effect, on Nat's mouth, and in the end Sayers was first down.

50. Sayers once more dashed in, but was met by Nat on the left peeper. Tom returned slightly on the body, and Langham again went to grass apparently weak.

51. Tom rushed in, delivered his left heavily on the conk, and then his right on the ribs without a return, and Nat dropped.

52. Tom again went to work, caught Langham on the side of his nut; Nat returned on the left peeper, and then slipped down.

53. Tom led off, got home on Langham's left eye, but the blow lacked force, and Nat fell, Sayers falling over him.

54. Sayers stepped in with his left, but was short; he tried it again, catching Nat on the waistband. Langham attempted a return, but Sayers jumped away. Nat again lunged out, but over-reaching himself, fell.

55. Nat seemed to shake himself together, went up to his man, led off with his left on the right cheek, and got away. Sayers followed him up, when some sharp exchanges took place, Nat reaching Tom's damaged snout, and once more

ON STRAIGHT HITTING. 83

turning on the tap. Tom returned the compliment on the left cheek, and Langham fell weak, Tom falling over him, not much better off.

56. It was now clear that Tom's peepers had not many minutes to remain open, and he therefore at once led off, but was out of distance; in a second attempt he caught Nat over the left peeper, but received another hot one on the nose in return. He would not be shaken off, however; he followed Nat and let fly his left on the jaw. Sharp counter-hits followed, Sayers on the mouth and nose, and Nat on the right ogle, and Langham fell.

57. Tom at once rushed in, but was stopped. His next effort reached Nat's mouth, and the latter got down.

58. Both were nearly pumped out, and it was evident that a chance hit might finish Langham, while Sayers if he could not deliver that hit must soon 'cut it.' The men let fly simultaneously, each getting it on the frontispiece. A break away followed, after which Tom reached Nat's left eye, but not effectively. A close, in which Tom caught his man with his right as he went down, and then fell on him.

59. Langham went to his man, delivered his left heavily on the nose, and received a little one on

the jaw. He then rushed at Sayers, who stepped back, and Nat, missing his mark, fell.

60. Sayers' fate was sealed; like Jack Broughton in the memorable account of Captain Godfrey, he might have exclaimed, 'I can't see my man; I'm blind, not beat. Only let me see my man, and he shall not gain the day yet.' Tom rushed in openhanded. Nat stepped on one side, met him as he came on the left peeper, and then beside the nose. Tom persevered, but Langham easily avoided him, and then popped him in the mouth heavily. Tom continued to bore in, and got in a round hit on the side of Nat's head, whereon Nat returned with his left just behind Tom's ear, and both fell. Sayers evidently all abroad.

61 and last. It was beyond a doubt now that Sayers could not see what he was doing or where he was going, and there were loud cries from his backers of 'Take him away,' which Alec Keene was anxious to do; but Tom, full of pluck as ever, resolutely refused to give in, and swinging his arms, walked deliberately to the scratch. He lunged out, but could not judge his distance, and Nat, waiting for him coolly until he came again, hit him heavily on the right eye. Poor Tom struck out wildly and altogether at random, and

Nat; getting out of his way, delivered a heavy left-hander on the left eye, which put up the other shutter, and he rather fell than was knocked down. On being helped to his corner, despite his entreaties, Alec Keene, seeing there was no hope, threw up the sponge, and Langham was proclaimed the victor in this truly gallant struggle, after a contest that had been protracted for two hours and two minutes. Immediately the fiat had been pronounced in his favour, Nat walked across the ring to shake hands with his defeated opponent, who shed bitter tears of disappointment and humiliation, while Nat, seeming to acquire fresh strength from the consciousness of victory, contrived to leap over the ropes, although five minutes before he could hardly stand on his legs."

After sustaining defeat at Nat Langham's hands, Tom Sayers seems to have steadily gone on improving, and many "big 'uns" went down before his all-conquering arm between 1853 and 1860, when "the Benicia Boy" tackled him.

It is probable that much of his success was due to the steady cultivation of a straight left, and, as in this case he had a man against him who stood four and a half inches over him, and was also a straight hitter, it will be seen that the gallant little Tom had plenty of scope for consummate tact and judgment, no less than bottom and gluttony in the matter of taking punishment.

SAYERS *v.* HEENAN.

The fight took place at Farnborough on April 17, 1860, and is thus described—

"*Round* 1. Heenan at once threw himself into very fair position, his left well balanced ready for a shoot, and the right across the body. Tom's position was the same as ever, lightly but firmly planted on his pins. He smiled and nodded, and on Heenan trying to lead off his left, got well back. Heenan tried again, his reach being tremendous, but again did Tom get well away. Tom now essayed a draw, but 'the Boy' was awake. Each feinted and dodged to find out a weak point, but for a short time each fortress was too well guarded. At last Tom let go his left and right, but out of distance. Heenan shook his nob and grinned, then again tried a lead, but was short. They got gradually to Heenan's corner, who appeared disposed to fight on the defensive, and the sun being in Tom's eyes seemed to bother him not a little. At length they came together, and sharp left-handers were exchanged, Tom getting on 'the Boy's' nose, drawing first blood, and Heenan leaving his sign-manual on Tom's frontispiece. Heavy counter-hits followed, Tom again getting on the nose, and receiving on the nob. More sparring ensued to a close, when Heenan seized Tom round the neck, but Tom pegged away at the back of his head until he made him leave that, and Tom fell laughing.

2. Heenan showed marks of Tom's handiwork on the back of his neck, and Tom's forehead was flushed. Heenan kept to his corner, whither Tom went to draw him out. When he thought Tom was near enough, 'the Boy' lunged out his left, but Tom stopped him and got back. Heenan tried again, and just reached Tom's nose. After one or two feints a pretty counter took place, Tom getting on the nose, and receiving a sharp one over the right eye. Heenan then closed, got well hold of him, and threw the Champion, falling heavily on him. Offers to take 2 to 1.

3. After a little lively fiddling, Tom got too near to the big 'un, who instantly slung out his left straight and full on the bridge of Tom's beak, knocking him clean off his pins. ('First knockdown' for Heenan.)

4. Tom, on coming up, looked rather astonished, and his eyes blinked in the sun like a dissipated owl. Heenan went at once to him at the scratch, dodged him, and once more planted a heavy spank with his left, this time on the jaw, and down went Tom again, amidst the shouts of the Yankees, who now offered 6 to 4 on Heenan. The Sayers party looked excessively blue.

5. Tom's mug showed visible marks of 'the Boy's' powers of hitting. He was cautious, and kept away from his man; Jack followed, and letting go his left on the mouth, was well countered by Tom on the proboscis. Heenan now bored in, and after dodging Tom, got again heavily on the sneezer, and Tom fell.

6. Tom's countenance, though not swelled, was much flushed, while 'the Boy' was almost scatheless. He was somewhat wild, and tried both hands, but missed. Counter-hits ensued, in which Tom received the full weight of Heenan's ponderous fist on his right arm, which was driven back against his face. Tom reached Heenan's left cheek, leaving his mark. Heenan retaliated on the right brow, and Tom fell.

7. Tom's right peeper displayed marks of pepper, and it was perceptible that he had sustained severe

injury to his right arm, which was beginning to swell, and which he now kept close to his body, as if to support it. Still he went to Heenan in his corner, and that hero delivered his left, but not effectively, on the chest. Tom danced away, and as he turned round, napped a little one from the right on his back. He was quickly out of harm's way, and, coming again, dodged his man, until he let fly, when Tom countered him heavily on the right cheek, drawing the claret and raising a considerable bump. The blow staggered Heenan, who stood all of a heap for a moment. Soon did he collect himself, and as Tom came again, lodged a little one on the nose, but was once more countered very heavily on the right cheek, the cut being increased and the bump enlarged. Slight exchanges followed, in which Tom received on the right eye, and Heenan on the right cheek, whereupon Heenan went to his corner for a sponge. He seemed in no hurry to come away, and Tom stood in the middle of the ring until Heenan went slowly to him, and tried his left, but it was no go. He tried again, but only just reached Tom's brow. Tom now feinted, and got home on the right peeper, Heenan missing an upper-cut. Tom danced away, came again on another track, and bang went his left on the sore spot, a heavy spank, and he was instantly out of danger, laughing; Heenan rushed after him, but was well stopped, thrice in succession. Again and again Tom went to him, and baulked his efforts to effect a lodgment, and then Heenan napped another slashing crack on the right cheek, which had the effect of at once closing his dexter goggle. He retreated for a wipe, and was followed by Tom, and some mutual cautious dodging and feinting took place. At last Heenan got on the top of Tom's smeller, but not heavily, and Tom then avoided another attempt. Once more did Heenan retire to Jack Macdonald for consolation and advice; Tom walking round and eyeing him in an inquisitive manner, as if admiring his handiwork. Tom, after satisfying his curiosity, went close, and slight exchanges followed, without mischief. Heenan tried his left, but was stopped. Both very cautious, and neither disposed to go within gunshot. Heenan now led off and got slightly on the mouth with his left, Tom retaliating on the closed peeper. Mutual taps and stops, and then Tom got his left heavily on the old spot, another cracker, whereupon Heenan once more retired into the privacy of his corner, amidst cries of 2 to 1 on Sayers. Tom, after a few turns and a

touch of the sponge, went to him, but Heenan
shook his nob, and seemed disinclined for work.
Tom, finding he could not draw him, retreated,
whereupon 'the Boy' came out, and let go his left
viciously, which was beautifully stopped. He then
feinted, and got well on the bridge of Tom's snorer
as he was retreating, and again knocked him off his
pins. Tom rolled over, laughing, and was carried
to his corner. This round lasted thirteen minutes,
and was a fine specimen of stratagem and skill,
especially on the part of Tom. His right arm now
was much swollen, and so painful that he could
make little or no use of it.

8. Tom slowest to the call of time, but directly
he was at the scratch 'the Boy' retired to his
corner, whither Tom had to follow him. Heenan
at once let go his left, but Tom laughed and
jumped back. A slight exchange followed, and
Tom napped a straight one on the sniffer. Heenan
now missed a couple of well-meant shots, and Tom
jumped away from a third, and as he turned his
back upon Heenan got a right-hander on the
back of the neck. Heenan followed him up, but
Tom grinned and jumped nimbly away. His
activity on his pins was as remarkable as ever.
Heenan pursued him, and at last lodged his left

slightly on the nozzle, and once more turned on the tap. Tom, however, countered him on the damaged cheek, which caused 'the Boy' to retire for the kind offices of Jack Macdonald. On Tom's going to him he let go his left on the kisser, drawing the carmine, and this led to pretty exchanges at long shots on the cheek. Heenan at this time appeared weak, and the hopes of the Sayers party were greatly in the ascendant. Heenan preferred his corner to the scratch, and Tom had some difficulty in persuading him to leave. This he at last accomplished, and some beautiful stops were made on both sides. Another break away ensued, after which they countered effectively, but Tom was heaviest on the right cheek, which was now swelled as big as two. Heenan's blow alighted on Tom's oration-trap, and drew more of the ruby. On his trying to repeat this lodgment, Tom stopped him cleverly. Capital exchanges followed, in which Tom was again at home on the cheek very heavily. Heenan rushed at him, but Tom was away, and, after once or twice being baulked, Heenan again retired to his corner. After Tom had scrutinized him carefully, he rubbed his hands and went to him, whereupon Heenan let fly his left, but Tom got well away laughing; Heenan shook his head and also laughed good-humouredly. Tom now crept in, and pop went his left on the plague-spot, and off went the Champion laughing. More dodging and stopping on both sides until Tom was once more on the cheek a slogger. Heenan retaliated sharply on the bridge of the snout, but was stopped in a second attempt, and Tom nailed him on the right cheek very heavily and got away. Heenan tried to take the lead, but Tom jumped back. 'The Boy,' persevering, got well on the forehead, but was unsuccessful in a second essay. The first was sufficient to leave a bump on the gallant Tom. More sparring until a severe counter-exchange took place, in which Tom got a hot 'un on the whistler, which shook his ivories and turned on a fresh tap. It was a staggerer, but Tom recovered and went to his man, when more severe counters were interchanged, Heenan getting another rum one on the cheek, and dropping his left with effect on Tom's sneezer. Both now indulged in a wipe, and washed their mouths out. They came again, now like giants refreshed, and each in turn tried a lead, but each was well stopped. Tom's right arm, from the continual stopping such a heavy cannonade as Heenan's, was now much discoloured and swollen, and utterly useless for all purposes of hitting, and he was thus deprived of his principal weapon. After a good deal of this another heavy exchange followed, in which Tom was at home on the old spot, and Heenan on the jaw heavily, knocking Tom once more off his pins. This round lasted twenty minutes, and was a splendid specimen of milling on both sides. Tom's nose and mouth were bleeding, but both his eyes were well open. His arm was his chief drawback. Heenan's right eye had been long closed, his cheek was fearfully swollen, and his mouth was somewhat out of straight.

9. Heenan came up as if he intended to force the fighting. He led off viciously, but Tom got well away. 'The Boy' followed him closely, and at last got on Tom's mouth, drawing more of the juice. He followed suit on the snuffer-tray with a like result, and counter-hits ensued, in which each did mischief. Heenan continued to bore in, and at last Tom, after getting a little one on the back, dropped, laughing.

10. Tom was very slow to the call of time, and appeared to want nursing. It was evidently heavy work struggling against such superior mettle. He stood in the middle of the ring until Heenan went to him, when slight counter-hits were exchanged;

ON STRAIGHT HITTING.

after which they closed. Heenan lifted Tom from the ground and threw him heavily with the greatest ease.

11. Tom again very much behind-hand in coming to time, and the friends of Heenan did not appear in much hurry. When they did come up Tom had to go into Heenan's corner. After a dodge or two Tom got his right on the good eye rather heavily, but it was not such a right-hander as of yore, and evidently gave him pain. Heenan returned on the chest, and Tom fell.

12. 'Time, time!' neither too ready. On Sayers at last facing his man, Heenan caught him, but not very heavily, on the jaw, and dropped on the saving suit.

13. Heenan, first to leave his second's knee, now went to Tom, and after a dodge or two popped the left very straight on Tom's nose, once more knocking him clean off his legs. He turned round on returning to his corner, and looking to Mr. Falkland, his umpire, exclaimed, 'That's one for you, Fred!' Offers were now made to lay 5 to 6 on Heenan, but the takers seemed scarce.

14. Tom, very weak, came up cautiously and slowly, his nose being large enough for two. Heenan, seeing Tom's state, tried to force the

fighting, but Tom got cleverly out of the difficulty. Heenan followed him up, and popped a rattler on the throat without a return. He paused, and then sent a little one on the scent-bottle, but Tom countered him well and straight on the nose, drawing the crimson in profusion. Heenan, nothing daunted, let go his left, and was stopped. He then swung round his right heavily on the jaw. They got to close quarters, and some heavy infighting took place, in which Tom was very busy. At length both were down heavily, Heenan under.

15. Neither seemed in a hurry to leave his second's knee, but Tom was slowest in answering the call. Heenan at once went to him, got the left well on the proboscis and his right on the jaw, and down again fell the Champion in a heap.

16. Tom shook himself together, but was very cautious. He sparred as if requiring rest, until Heenan came in, when slight exchanges took place, Tom getting it on the nose and Heenan on the whistler, but neither very heavily. Heenan then made a sudden dart, and planting heavily on Tom's mouth, once more knocked him off his legs. (Loud cheers for Heenan.)

17. Tom did not display many marks from his repeated knock-down blows, but came up smiling,

ON STRAIGHT HITTING.

although somewhat tired. Heenan's mug was decidedly the most disfigured, being so much swelled. Heenan took the lead, but did not get heavily on. He tried again with his right, but the blow passed over Tom's nob. Counter hits followed on the nose, in which Tom's delivery was most effective, but Tom was down.

18. Very slight exchanges, followed by a heavy counter, in which Heenan's mouth came in for pepper, and Tom got it slightly on the nose, and fell.

19. Tom slow to time; Heenan not in a hurry. At last, on facing one another, Heenan went in to a close, and throwing Tom, fell on him.

20. Heenan followed Sayers, who was on the retreat, and after one or two dodges, caught him heavily on the jaw with his right. He tried again, but Tom jumped back. Still he persevered, and heavy exchanges followed at close quarters, and both were in the end down at the ropes.

21. Sayers very slow, which Heenan seeing, dashed at him, slung out the left on the nose, and again floored the Champion.

22. Tom seemed none the worse for his floorer; it rather seemed to do him good, for he became fresher, which Heenan seeing, he retired to his

corner. Tom followed and tried to deliver, but missed, and the Benicia Boy dropped him with another straight one on the jaw. Heenan's left hand was now much puffed, and did not seem to leave such impressions as formerly.

23. The time was very badly kept on both sides, and there were now complaints that the Benicia Boy was allowed a stool in the ring. An appeal was made to the referee, who at once ordered its removal, as contrary to the laws. Heenan rushed at Tom, who retreated and got one on the back. Tom then turned round, and missed his right. They closed, and Tom pegged away merrily on the nose and left cheek, and in the end both down, Tom under. One hour and eleven minutes had now elapsed.

24. The Benicia Boy, first up, tried his left by a sudden dart, but was stopped. An attempt with the right just landed on the side of Tom's nut, and he fell. (5 to 4 on Heenan still offered.)

25. Tom weak, came up slow, but cheerful. He waited the attack, which was not long in coming, and after getting a little one on the side of his head, Tom popped his left very heavily on the snout, drawing more home-brewed. Heenan, wild, rushed in and bored Tom down.

26. Tom, fresher, came up gaily, and tried to land off with his left, but 'the Boy' stopped him prettily. Another effort landed on Heenan's good eye. Heenan in return planted a rattler on Tom's jaw with his right, which staggered him, and was all but a knock down. Tom soon shook himself together, whereupon Heenan let fly his left, but Tom was well away. Following up, 'the Boy' got on Tom's chest, but not heavily. Exchanges; Heenan on the 'tato-trap, and Tom on the nose, a smasher, each drawing the cork. Heavy counters followed with the left, and they broke away. Heenan came again, and got on Tom's snorer heavily with his left, once more staggering him. Twice after this did Tom stop Heenan's right, and they closed. After some slight fibbing Tom fell, Heenan hitting him when down. An appeal of foul was overruled, the blow being obviously accidental.

27. 'The Boy' came up determined and led off, but Tom was away. A second attempt was equally unsuccessful, and as Tom turned his back to dash away, 'the Boy' caught him on the neck, but not heavily. Sharp exchanges followed, Tom on the left cheek and nose, and 'the Boy' on the mouth. Heenan then went in and tried his left,

but was short, whereupon he retired to his corner, had a wipe, and wetted his whistle, and then went to the middle of the ring. Tom joined issue at once, and some heavy exchanges took place, each on the nose, and Heenan now tried to close, reaching after Tom to catch him round the neck. Tom kept out of harm's way, but at length 'the Boy' bored him down at the ropes.

28. Both, much fatigued, wanted all the time they could get. After some sparring, Heenan ran at Tom, who darted away. 'The Boy' rapidly pursued, and they got together, and in the fibbing Tom was busy on Heenan's good cheek, while he caught it on the mouth. In the end Tom was down.

29. Tom still slow to time. 'The Boy' at once went to him and got heavily on the top of his nut. Tom countered with effect with his right on the left cheek, and then popped his left on the proboscis. Heavy exchanges followed in Tom's favour, who met 'the Boy' very straight and effectively on the nozzle, opening a fresh bin. A break away, followed by slight exchanges, led to a harmless close, and Tom slipped down.

30. Heenan's other eye was now quickly closing, and he had evidently no time to lose. He was

strongest on his legs, but his punishment was far more visible than Tom's. He tried to lead off, but Tom met him neatly on the nose, turning on the red port. 'The Boy' rushed at Tom, and literally ran over and fell on him.

31. After standing some time in his corner, Heenan was fetched out by Tom, who had now recovered a little. A short spar was followed by another retreat, after which Tom went in and got a little 'un on the left cheek, but it lacked steam. More sparring, and Heenan again retired. Tom stood and examined him with the eye of a connoisseur until he came out, when good exchanges took place, Tom getting heavily on the mouth, and Heenan on the nose. A break away; more sparring for wind; Heenan again to his corner. On Tom going at him he slung out his left heavily on the nose, and prone once more fell the brave Champion.

32. Tom, all alive, dodged, and caught 'the Boy' on the chin. He turned to retreat, and 'the Boy' nailed him on the body, but not heavily. Heenan then tried repeatedly to draw Tom, but the latter would not go into Heenan's corner. 'The Boy,' therefore, had to go out, and some rapid hits and stops followed, without any apparent damage;

each, however, got a small tap on the mouth. Heenan having taken another rest in his corner, came out, and got a hot one on his left cheek for his pains, which all but shut up the other eye. This brought on exchanges, each on the mazzard, and then Heenan reached Tom's nose. Heavy determined counter deliveries on the nose ensued, after which Heenan floored Tom by a right-hander on the cheek. The betting was now even, Sayers for choice. It was obvious, that strong as Heenan was, unless he could make a decided change, he must in a very few minutes be blind.

33. The Benicia Boy feeling he had no time to lose, rushed in, but only just reached Tom's chest. Both seemed fagged, and they stood a few seconds, and then went to close quarters, where Tom, as usual, was busy on 'the Boy's' frontispiece, until he let him slip through his arms on to the ground.

34. Heenan again tried to force the fighting, but Tom got away. They then stood and sparred until Heenan let fly his left, which did not reach its destination. He retired for counsel, and then came at Tom and tried his right at the body, but without success. Steady exchanges led to a close and rapid in-fighting, and both fell, Tom under. Heenan's eye all but closed up.

35. The Benicia Boy dashed viciously in, and caught Tom on the snout, but the blow was without power. Tom retreated from the vigorous onslaught; Heenan followed and got home on the jaw with the right, still with no effect. Tom now turned and ran, Heenan after him, when, on turning round, Tom napped one on the nose. He, however, landed another little pop on the good eye. Sharp exchanges at close quarters ended in the downfall of Tom. Two hours had now elapsed.

36. The Benicia Boy's face was a spectacle to behold, while Tom was very weak. 'The Boy' rushed to a close, and caught Tom round the neck, dragging him to the ropes. At this time, the police, who had been gradually making their way to the ring, began a violent struggle to get close and put a stop to hostilities. 'The Boy' tried to hold Tom, but the latter slipped through his arms and fell.

37. Tom was first up, and seemed the better man; he made his left twice on Heenan's eye, and the latter at length caught him round the neck at the ropes and there held him. Tom's efforts to extricate himself were in vain, but he administered severe punishment on Heenan's face. The police

at this time got closer, there was a rush to the ropes from all sides, and we, in company with others, including the referee, were completely shut out from the view. We are informed that the round ended in both going to grass at the expiration of two hours and six minutes. We had hoped that the men would have been withdrawn, as the referee had been forced from his post and the police were close by. The battle, so far as it may be called a battle, was for the time over, and the men should have been taken away. However, although the referee sent orders for a cessation of hostilities, five more so-called rounds were fought, with pretty equal advantage. Heenan's right eye was fast closing, his left being in complete darkness. The ring was half full of people, however, and neither man had a fair chance. Much do we regret the unpleasant duty that now is imposed on us, of finding fault with the Benicia Boy for conduct which was not only unmanly, but quite against the rules of the Ring, and had the referee been present would inevitably have lost him the battle. We can ourselves declare, as an impartial eye-witness of the *mêlée*, that in the fourth of these supplementary rounds, while Sayers was on his second's knee, Heenan rushed at him in a very excited state, let fly left and right at Tom's seconds, floored them, and kicked at them when on the ground in desperate style, after which he closed with Sayers, and after a wild rally, they fell together. The final round was merely a wild scramble, in which both fell. The referee by this time was able to get near again, and ordered the men to desist from fighting. Immediately after this Heenan rushed away from the ring, and ran some distance with the activity of a deer, proving that as far as strength was concerned, he was as fit as ever; but he had not been from the ring many minutes before he was totally blind. Tom Sayers, although a little tired, and suffering from his arm and that desperate hug in the thirty-seventh round, was also very strong on his pins, and could have fought some time longer. The Blues were now in force; there was of course no chance for the men again meeting, and an adjournment was necessary. It was found that the authorities were up in arms in all directions, so that it would be mere waste of time to go elsewhere. Backward home was therefore the word, and the men and their friends returned to the Metropolis shortly after three o'clock. The whole time occupied, up to the men's leaving the ring, was two hours and twenty minutes."

After a perusal of the various fights in which Tom Sayers figured with almost invariable success, one is impressed by two things, viz. the excellency of his judgment, and his partiality for the "double" lead with the left. It is probable that the first "show" was often a feint, and that the hit was intended as it came off; but he very often led at the body with the left, and instantly followed up the hit with a second in the face with the same hand.

In his fight with the Tipton Slasher (*vide* preceding chapter) he frequently used the double, and no doubt with great effect.

A very good lead is at the body with the right, instantly followed up by the left at the head, or, if boxing with a right-handed boxer, with the left at the body and right at the head.

Just before your lead off it is often well to gain a few inches by drawing up the right foot very slightly, and so that the adversary may not suspect your intention. You will thus gain your distance without springing off the ground at all with the right foot: at the effective moment of the hit, *i.e.* when your fist has reached the opponent's head, the right foot should still be firmly planted on the ground, or at any rate the ball of the foot should be there.

As in retreating, it is a great mistake to ever have both feet off the ground *at the same time*, and "springs" should not be resorted to unless in a very tight place, and when it is desirable to get right away from an almost hopeless difficulty.

The advancing of the right foot may be aptly called "creeping" nearer to your man, and it is wonderful how even an inch or two gained in this way will help in your lead.

In making use of the double leads with both hands a good deal of confidence is needed, for you have to get in nearer to your man, and so run more risk of counters. For example, suppose you are leading off with the doubles left and right at body and head; it is true that the adversary will probably employ his right in guarding his body, but he will probably shoot his left bang at your head at the same time, so that in this double you must be careful to duck well to the left and endeavour to shoot out your right and catch him under the jaw.

These double leads should be executed with great rapidity and boldness, as with a smart left-hander like Nat Langham, for example, we always have the left shooting out, and the movement is then attended with danger. It will be better to keep to the left-hand leads and left-hand doubles entirely for some years, and hold the right in reserve. (*Vide* Chapter IX.)

GUARD FOR RIGHT-HAND BODY BLOW.

CHAPTER V.

HALF-ARM OR ROUND HITS.

MANY short, thick-set men who are poor hands at long leads and straight-hitting, may become formidable antagonists at close quarters. At all-distance work, the weight of the body is far more thrown into the blow than when the short-arm hits are used.

As previously mentioned, a hit should not be swung round with a bent arm except when at close quarters, and then the arm and fore-arm should be at right angles to one another so as to get most force out of the hit; it will be seen that in this class of blow more depends upon the power of the muscles than the weight of the body. These hits are of great importance, and should not be neglected, but since they are more easily learnt they need not be practised so often as the long leads.

The "hook hit" is advocated by some teachers, and there is no doubt that severe blows may be dealt with it, *e.g.* knock-out hit on side of head. As the arm is partially bent it is not possible to reach as far as with the straight arm; but the gravest objection to this hit is that you run such a chance of breaking or disabling your own arm through contact with the opponent's shoulder or elbow. Proofs that many men have become so disabled through the use of this very hit will be found in the history of the Ring. It will reach a man at a greater distance than the true "contracted arm," but it lacks the "punch" there is behind the straight hit, and is not as forcible as the true half-arm blow.

A wide distinction must be drawn between the turn of the hand when delivering the cross-counter, of which more anon, and this, to my mind, highly objectionable hook hit. Of course when you are dealing with a beaten man, and he is standing in an exhausted condition with hands down, you can polish him off with any kind of a hit—hook or otherwise; but why not use a legitimate hit such as a good straight left or right well under the chin?

Though you should not make use of the hook hit yourself, you should know how to deal with a man who does use it. It is a hit which tends to twist its exponent round, and if you can avoid the blow you can encourage the twisting by stepping in and delivering a crusher on the side of the head.

The "upper cut" is an excellent stop for an opponent who rushes in with his head down, but it is wonderful how often it misses its mark altogether, and it is therefore advisable to practise it as often as possible on rough-and-tumble fighters, labourers, farm hands, etc. It is delivered vertically upwards, with the arm well bent, and, at close quarters, with either hand, but more usually with the right. When it comes off satisfactorily it is very useful, as the adversary occasionally falls to the ground face downward, and anyhow he gets a nasty jerk which will make him more careful how he rushes in.

Sometimes, when in a rough fight, it will be well to avoid a left-hand lead by a duck slightly to the right, and at the same time stoop well down and run the point of your left shoulder well into your opponent's left ribs. This may knock some of the wind out of him, and possibly break a rib or two, but it is an expedient only to be resorted to in rough quarters, and is not allowed in competitions.

It is mentioned here because it is one of the many artifices used in " in-fighting."

A confirmed "rusher" invariably hits round, and often turns his back to you, so that if you are smart you can often get in a hit on his short ribs near the spine and just above the belt. This is called the kidney hit, and is more effective with the naked fist than with the boxing-gloves; it is to be reckoned amongst the dangerous hits on account of the serious results it sometimes brings about.

It will be well, as soon as you have made a fair advance in the comprehension of general principles, to practise in-fighting on account of its frequent use in actual fights, and with the object of ascertaining, as far as possible, where the wrestler's art encroaches on the domain of pugilism. Clinches, catches, hipes, back-heels, cross-buttocks, flying-buttocks, back-falls, etc. are properly not permitted; but the rough who suddenly attacks you in the street won't consider all this—he will kick, bite, seize hold of *any* portion of your anatomy, and, if opportunity offers, gouge out your eye.

So you cannot know too much about wrestling.

The boxing keeps your man at a distance: when, however, he gets to close quarters, short-arm hits

HALF-ARM OR ROUND HITS.

and wrestling will be necessary if he is to be properly disposed of.

For example, suppose a rough fellow gets your head "in chancery," you may either set to work punching him with *both* your hands on his mark

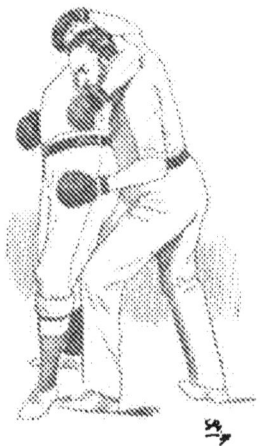

Fig. 3. The Back-Fall.

and short ribs, or you may suddenly bring one of your hands round his back and under his chin, force back his head, and throw him on your knee, as shown in Fig. 3. This is called the "back-fall," and if quickly executed is a capital reply to the head-in-chancery position.

The "cross-buttock" and "flying-buttock" may

both arise out of the head-in-chancery. Your opponent, having got you in chancery, swings his hips round, throws you over them in a heap on the ground, and then falls on you. This is a very dangerous throw, and is easily executed by a stronger and heavier man unless you at once resort to some satisfactory stop.

Fig. 4. The Back-Heel.

In the "back-heel" we have a most excellent throw, and it very often arises like this :—Your opponent may have shot his left over your *right* shoulder; you hold his arm in that position with your right, push his head back with your left hand, and at the same time strike the back part of his left leg, just below the knee, with your left heel.

HALF-ARM OR ROUND HITS.

If this is done smartly, and you simultaneously release his left arm, he will be thrown heavily on his back.

The reply or stop for the back-heel is to throw the right leg well back so as to increase the stability, and at the same time to advance the head

Fig. 5. Stop for Cross-Buttock.

and body as much as possible against the push which is intended to produce the fall.

"Rushers" are always delightful men to tackle, as they really do more than half the work themselves. Like the disappointed Roman falling on his sword, the rusher hurls his weight against your fist. Remember then that when your rusher happens to be taller than yourself, and is coming straight for you, duck slightly to avoid his hits, and let him have the contracted arm with the left on the mark, and immediately afterwards follow this up with the contracted arm with the right on his short ribs. Then instantly break away to the right, and be ready to meet him with a straight left.

In a future chapter the question of dangerous hits will be considered more fully, but whilst on the subject of body-blows, I think it well to give an account, taken from the *Mirror of Life*, of the most important fight of the present year. I allude of course to the great contest between Corbett and Fitzsimmons, which was decided by the terrific body-hits of the Cornishman.

CORBETT *v.* FITZSIMMONS.

The fight took place at Carson City, Nevada, U.S.A., on St. Patrick's Day, 1897, and is thus described—

"The ring was raised about 4ft. above the level of the floor, and the iron posts at each corner were carefully bound up with cotton batting. The floor of the ring was of inch pine boards, closely drawn together, and liberally sprinkled with resin. The boards were bare. William Muldoon, the famous wrestler and trainer, was the official timekeeper. Louis Houseman, of Chicago, held the watch for the Australian, while James Colville performed a like office for Corbett. George Siler, of Chicago, was referee. Five-ounce gloves were used. Corbett, who won the toss yesterday, chose the south-east corner, with his back to the sun. The men entered the ring a few minutes before twelve, and immediately stripped. Fitzsimmons looked light, but was a perfect bunch of muscles. Corbett looked easily 15lbs. heavier, and his skin, as well as that of Fitzsimmons, shone like polished mahogany. Fitzsimmons refused to shake hands with his opponent. Time was called at seven minutes past twelve.

Round 1. Sparring for an opening, Fitzsimmons forced Corbett to his corner. He tried a left swing, which Jem ducked cleverly. Jem meanwhile was smiling, but Fitzsimmons was very aggressive. He landed lightly on Corbett's neck. Jem feinted, and landed a left hook on his opponent's stomach, following this up with a left hook on Fitzsimmons' jaw. The men clinched, but no damage was done. In the break away, Corbett next landed a right swing on his antagonist's ribs. A second clinch again resulted in no damage. In the break away Fitzsimmons landed with his left on Jem's head, and Corbett landed with his right on Fitzsimmons' short ribs. Another clinch followed, and Fitzsimmons landed heavily with his right on Corbett's head. Jem laughed, and landed again with his right on Fitzsimmons' ribs, when the gong ended the round.

Coming up for the second round Corbett advanced to the centre and clinched, but no damage resulted. In the break away more clinching followed. Corbett was very cautious, and kept a keen look-out for the slightest opening. He landed two stiff left swings on his opponent's head. Fitzsimmons swung with his left and right, and landed lightly on Corbett's head. The fighting now became very rapid, both being extremely lively on their feet. Jem landed hard with his left on Fitzsimmons' stomach, and followed with another on the same place. He was jabbing Fitzsimmons hard with his right and left on the body when the bell rang.

In the third round Corbett started with his right, and got in with a hard left hook on the body. Fitzsimmons became savage, and tried with his left and right at Corbett's head, but did very little damage. Corbett landed another left jab on the body, following it up with a right short on the ribs. Jem clinched, and landed with his right hard over the heart. Fitzsimmons mixed it up, and put the heel of his glove in Corbett's face. In the clinch Jem kept his right working like a piston-rod on Fitzsimmons' body. They clinched, and Fitzsimmons roughed it in the break away. As the gong sounded, Fitzsimmons seemed anxious to continue; but Corbett, laughing, stuck his right glove in his opponent's face, and they retired to their corners.

Coming up for the fourth round Corbett, rushing in, landed his left again on Fitzsimmons' body. The latter was short with his left. Fitzsimmons followed with a stiff left on Jem's stomach, and they clinched. Fitzsimmons roughed it again. They were now fighting at a terrific rate, and making a magnificent contest. Fitzsimmons rushed, and Jem met him with a stiff right-hand short blow on the stomach. Fitzsimmons was now doing a good deal of rushing and hitting, and roughing it in the break aways. It now looked long odds on Corbett making a clever fight of it. He was playing systematically with his right and left on the body. An exchange of lefts at the head followed, and time was called.

In the fifth round Corbett landed with his left on Fitzsimmons' jaw. Immediately again Jem's left went on his opponent's jaw. The blows dealt by Fitzsimmons had plenty of steam behind them, but they were not so frequent as Corbett's. They clinched and exchanged compliments with one arm loose. Corbett led with a very slow left, and Fitzsimmons landed with his left on Jem's neck. The latter threw a stiff half-round blow with his left on his antagonist's nose, drawing first blood. They mixed, and Corbett had the better of it. Jem landed another stiff right on the body and a left on the chin. This round ended in favour of Corbett.

In the sixth round the men clinched, and Fitzsimmons tried to wrestle Corbett down. There were loud cries of 'Oh, oh!' Corbett landed lightly with a left jab on the face, Fitzsimmons countering on the jaw. Corbett upper-cut. Corbett struck Fitzsimmons fiercely with his right, and had him going down. Fitzsimmons was now literally covered with blood, but was fighting like a demon. Corbett was beginning to show signs of the fast work. Fitzsimmons was down on one knee, and took the time limit; but he was full of fight on getting up again. Corbett, however, was simply slaughtering him with his upper-cuts. At the same time Jem's leads were wild, and he missed many well-intentioned blows. When time was called, Fitzsimmons looked very much the worse for wear, and Corbett was puffing a lot.

In the seventh round Corbett now forced the fight. He missed a left swing at the head, but upper-cut Fitzsimmons hard on the face. Fitzsimmons was bleeding again, but fighting hard. Both men were now looking for a knock-out blow. Jem landed a light left on Fitzsimmons' now sore mouth. Fitzsimmons missed right and left swings, then tried another left swing, which Corbett ducked. Jem countered with a heavy right over the heart. Corbett now looked very tired, and Fitzsimmons was bleeding like a stuck bullock. He, nevertheless, looked as strong as his opponent. When the men started for the eighth round Fitzsimmons forced the fight. An exchange of blows did very little damage. Fitzsimmons missed a left swing, and was lifted off his feet by a straight left jab from Corbett on the mouth. Fitzsimmons did all the forcing in this round. He tried a right-hand cross, but Corbett ducked. Fitzsimmons landed with his left on Corbett's face, and Jem countered with his right on the body. The combatants sparred for wind. Fitzsimmons tried his right hard at Corbett's head, but was countered heavily on the jaw with a good left from Corbett. Fitzsimmons had the worst of this round.

In the ninth round began some long-range sparring. Both men were still very active on their feet. Fitzsimmons landed below the belt, and was cautioned by the referee. Corbett landed a stiff left on his opponent's wind. Fitzsimmons rushed Corbett, but did very little damage. Corbett was jabbing, clinching, and upper-cutting with his right. In the break away Fitzsimmons landed very hard with a left-hand swing on Jem's jaw, and tried a right cross, but Jem was inside. Fitzsimmons again tried a right cross, but was short. He was now, however, landing more frequently than Corbett, and when the men started for the tenth round Fitz held a decided advantage. In this round Fitzsimmons was spitting blood. He tried a hard left swing at Corbett's head, and came back with a stiff left and right on Corbett's head and body. At this stage he appeared to be very much cooler and stronger than Corbett. The latter stopped a left swing with a straight left on the mouth. Fitzsimmons meanwhile was bleeding profusely, but he forced Corbett back, being apparently the stronger man. They mixed it up, and honours were about even, both fighting hard, when Fitzsimmons caught Corbett round the neck and dragged him to the ropes, when time was called.

In the eleventh round Corbett landed a light left on Fitzsimmons' mouth. His blow lacked force, but he was still fighting very cautiously. A clinch followed. Corbett landed with his right on the ribs, and was countered with a left jab on the chin. Fitzsimmons was now receiving many of Corbett's left jabs, but he looked as strong as a bear. Corbett missed a half-round hook on the jaw, and Fitzsimmons landed a hard left straight on Corbett's face. They clinched, and Fitzsimmons crossed with his right. They mixed it, and Fitzsimmons had decidedly the better of the roughing. He fought Corbett to his corner, and had him weak as the gong sounded.

Coming up for round 12, Corbett rushed it. He missed with his left, and was countered on the face. It was evident that Fitzsimmons was now bent on rushing it, and Corbett kept away. Fitzsimmons got the worst of it in the rush. There was more clinching, and Corbett landed with his left on his opponent's nose, following with a half-round at the body. Corbett forced Fitzsimmons' to the ropes, and smashed hard on his short ribs. It was now Corbett who was rushing. He landed one or two rights and lefts on the Australian's face. He again landed with his left on Fitzsimmons' face, and followed with a right on the body. He then tried for a knock-out with an upper-cut with his right, but it was too short. The round ended in favour of Corbett.

Round 13 saw Fitzsimmons as strong as a lion. He landed a right short on Corbett's ribs, and a left on the jaw. Jem next found Fitzsimmons with a good left. Fitzsimmons rushed with him over to his corner, but did very little damage. Corbett jabbed Fitzsimmons lightly on the head, and again on the body. Corbett at this stage was sparring beautifully, and ducking some dangerous blows. Fitzsimmons landed with his left straight and hard on Jem's face. He then tried a hard right swing, but did no good. Jem's glove was in Fitzsimmons' face when time was called.

Round 14 and last. In this round Corbett led, but was baulked. He then landed a left jab again on Fitzsimmons' head. Fitzsimmons countered with a terrible right swing on Corbett's neck, and

RIGHT-HANDED BODY BLOW.

had Corbett going back for a few moments. Fitzsimmons next landed a terrible left-hand jab on Corbett's stomach, and Corbett went to his knees with a frightful look of agony on his face. The timekeepers called ten seconds. But Corbett came to his feet, rushed to Fitzsimmons, and endeavoured to strike. A terrible uproar ensued, but the referee decided that Fitzsimmons had won. The punch that did the business landed over Jem Corbett's heart, and he collapsed."

After such an important fight there were, as may be readily supposed, plenty of different versions and accounts flying about—no event of the kind has ever been decided without a great many excuses, explanations, and arguments.

According to some witnesses the right-handed blow over the heart did the mischief, but it seems more probable the left-hand tucked-in smasher on the "mark" lost Corbett the championship. Mr. G. Siler, the referee, took this view, for he is reported to have said—"It was a fair, square, and manly fight, and in my judgment the best man won. No foul was committed. Fitzsimmons simply stepped in close, swung his left hard into the pit of the stomach, quickly following it with his right over the heart. It was the former blow, however, that gave Fitz the world's championship. It doubled Jem up completely and took his breath away. Fitz quickly saw that Corbett was done for, and, although I naturally stepped in to see that no foul was committed, Fitz never for a moment lost his head. It was a good, clean fight, and I think will do much toward making boxing popular throughout the Union."

It would be hardly fair to quote the remarks of the victor and the vanquished, since they were necessarily made in circumstances of great excitement. There was no question about the genuineness of the contest; each did his level best to win, and, as in the case of the great Sayers and Heenan fight, a middle weight showed his gameness and stamina.

As the question of rushing in has been more than once alluded to in this chapter, it will perhaps be interesting to here give an account of a pluckily contested old-time fight, where the bigger man did a great deal of the leading, exhausted himself by his efforts, and added to his own punishment by persistently and recklessly boring in on an opponent whose good left hand carried him victoriously through dozens of fights. The account of this fight, as given in *Pugilistica*, bristles with quaint expressions, and the phraseology of the Ring is much to the fore.

Of the great little Tom Sayers it was said that his star as a champion at 10st. 10lbs. was rapidly rising in the year 1856. He had polished off the middle weights, and had been playing havoc among the heavies: these tactics he managed to pursue to the close of his career, when he had the satisfaction of being able to say that he was only *once* beaten, and then by his brother middle weight, Nat Langham.

The fight with Tom Paddock given below came off on Cauvey Island on June 16, 1858.

TOM SAYERS *v.* TOM PADDOCK.

"*Round* 1. Both came grinning to the scratch, and manœuvred for a brief space for an opening. Paddock looked, as usual, big and burly, but it was evident he was no longer the active fresh man we had before seen. His mug was more marked with age, and there was a dulness about his eye we never remember in former days. His condition was good, as he was in good health, but still he looked only Tom Paddock in name. Sayers was more fleshy than he should have been, but this was the only fault to be found with him. His eye was as bright and clear as a hawk's, and the ease of his movements was a picture to behold. His attitude was, as usual, all readiness for a shoot or a jump. Paddock, instead of rushing, as had been expected, steadied himself, and felt with his left for an opening. It was not long before he attempted it, but Sayers stopped him easily. He made a second attempt, and Sayers stepped back, shaking his noddle and laughing. After a little sparring Paddock tried again, and got on Tom's brow, but not heavily. Again they dodged, and at length two counter-hits were exchanged, each getting on to the proboscis. After this Paddock again reached Tom's nozzle rather sharply, but was stopped in another attempt. Another bit of cautious sparring eventually led to very heavy exchanges, in which Sayers left a mark on Paddock's left cheek, and napped a warm one over the right peeper, slightly removing the bark, and giving Paddock the first event. Several rapid passes were now made on both sides, but they were evidently mere trials to find out what each intended. After a pause, Sayers tried his favourite double, which he succeeded in landing on Paddock's cheek, but not very heavily.

More sharp exchanges followed, the advantage being with Sayers, until they both retreated and stood to cool themselves, the heat being intense. After a few seconds thus employed, they again approached one another smiling, and after a dodge or two they exchanged slight reminders on the side of the nut, broke away, and then got at it again, when heavy counter-hits were exchanged, but Sayers was first, and inflicted a cut on Paddock's left brow, calling forth the juice in abundance. Paddock landed on the cheek, but not heavily. After this slight exchanges with the left took place, and they again stood, Sayers awaiting the onslaught, and Paddock puzzled. At last the latter dashed in, and was easily stopped twice in succession. He rushed after Sayers, who ducked under his arm, and, as Paddock turned round again, nailed him very heavily over the left peeper, renewed the supply of carmine, and then got out of harm's way. Paddock, nothing daunted, dashed in, but Sayers stopped him most beautifully, and then putting in his double, got well on the old spot. Paddock once more bored in, and was neatly stopped, but, persevering with his usual gameness, heavy exchanges ensued, all in favour of Sayers, who was as straight as a die, and got heavily on the left cheek and brow. Paddock, wild, rushed after him; Sayers ducked, and then planted his left on the left cheek, another hot one, and then on the snout, renewing the ruby. As Paddock bored in, he made a cannon off the cushion by putting his double heavily on the mark and nose without a return, and Paddock then rushing after him, bored him down. This round lasted fifteen minutes, and at its conclusion the backers of Sayers offered 2 to 1—an offer not accepted by the Paddock party, who looked indigo. It was patent to all good judges even thus early that Paddock was only Paddock in name, and that all the steel was out of him; and he has since informed us that he felt tired and worn out, and that he had no chance from this time. His gameness, therefore, in persevering so long and so manfully against his own conviction is the more commendable.

2. Both came up grinning, but while Sayers was almost scatheless, Paddock's mug showed that Sayers had been there. Paddock, nothing daunted, rattled in, and got on to the top of Tom's nob; Sayers returned, but not heavily, and sharp counter-hits followed, Sayers on the damaged ogle, and Paddock on the left cheek. After this, Sayers got

home his dangerous right on the side of Paddock's nob, and the latter fell.

3. Paddock seemed slow, while Sayers was as fresh as a daisy; Paddock attempted to lead, but was very short. He, however, stopped Tom's return. Heavy exchanges followed, Sayers receiving on the left cheek, and getting heavily on Paddock's damaged squinter. Paddock, nothing daunted, made several desperate efforts, but Sayers got away with the greatest ease, and at length, as Paddock persevered, he was once more countered on the old spot, drawing more of the red port, and stopped Paddock's return. Twice again did Sayers repeat this visitation, and get away from Paddock's kindly intentions. Sayers then tried to lead off, but was well stopped. He made another attempt, and lodged his favourite double on the mark and nose, and then stopped Paddock's return. Paddock now endeavoured to force the fighting, but Sayers danced away under his arm, came again, and as Paddock rushed in, delivered a tremendous left-hander on the cheek by the side of the smeller, drawing more home-brewed from the fresh cut. Paddock, angry, made several desperate efforts, but was well stopped. At length they got close, and in the heavy exchanges, Sayers got his right

heavily on the side of the nut, and received on the mouth. Paddock now dashed in, and although Sayers pinked him on the nose and eye, he persevered until he forced Sayers down.

4. Paddock's physog. seemed a good deal out of the line of beauty, while Sayers had scarcely a mark. Paddock still smiled, and attempted to lead, but the dash and vigour we remember of yore were all gone; his blows seemed but half-arm hits, and did not get near their destination. Almost every time Sayers stopped him with ease, and at last, as Paddock came boring in, he met him heavily on the cheek, producing another streak of cochineal. Still did Paddock persevere, but only to be nailed again, and to have the Red Republican once more called forth. After this he got home on Tom's chest, and then on the cheek, but the blows lacked vigour. Exchanges ensued, in which Paddock removed the bark from Tom's sniffer, and turned on the main, but it was not a material damage. After a rest, in which both piped for wind, they again got at it, and a tremendous rally took place, in which Sayers was straightest and heaviest; he, however, got a hot 'un on the mouth, which drew the Badminton. This was a tremendous give-and-take round, and

Paddock caught it heavily on the left side of his nob, while Sayers received chiefly on the hardest parts of his cast-iron canister. In the end Paddock was down, amidst the vociferous cheers of the Sayers party.

5. Paddock made two ineffectual attempts to deliver, each being short, after which Sayers missed his favourite double. He then stopped Paddock's one, two, and exchanges followed, in which Paddock reached Tom's chin, and received with interest on the damaged cheek. Again did they deliver left and right, and Paddock drew more gravy from Tom's sucker. Paddock rattled to it, but Sayers countered heavily on the snorer, again calling forth the ruby; he, however, napped one on the kisser, which must have shaken his false ivories. After this they piped for wind, the perspiration oozed from every pore, and they were evidently both tired. Paddock retired for a wipe, and after a pause Sayers went to him, and Paddock seeing this rushed in, but Tom danced away, followed by Paddock, who eventually got a reminder on the cheek, and Sayers in getting away from the return, fell.

6. Sayers feinted and dodged until Paddock came to him, when Tom got home a very hot one

on the snuff-box, turning on the vermilion galore. Paddock, wild, dashed at him to deliver his right, but Sayers getting quickly out of mischief, the blow fell on the stake, and evidently caused the poor fellow intense pain. He was not cowed, however, but followed Sayers, who fell, and Paddock's umpire appealing, the referee desired Sayers to be cautious.

7. Paddock, slow, came up cautiously, and after a few dodges led off, but was short, and received a reminder on the beak from Tom's left. Sayers then got heavily on the mark with the left, and stopped the return. This led to heavy exchanges, in which Paddock received on the nose, and lost more juice, while Sayers only got it on the brow. Paddock tried again and again to lead off, but Sayers danced away, or ducked under his arm, and each time nailed him heavily on the nose or left cheek, and finally Paddock fell weak.

8. Paddock's left peeper was now completely closed, and the left side of his knowledge-box much swollen. He was sent up very clean, however, and again tried to lead off, but Sayers was too quick for him and got away. Still did the gallant Paddock persevere, but Sayers stopped him with ease, and returned on the damaged visual

organ very heavily. Paddock again dashed in, but was short, his blows lacking vigour; and Sayers returned on the mark. Again and again did Paddock make an onslaught, but there was none of the vigour of the Paddock of former days; he was repeatedly stopped with ease, and Sayers caught him again and again on the mark and damaged chop. At last they got close together, and Paddock succeeded in knocking Sayers off his pins by a heavy right-hander on the whistler, which inflicted a severe cut, and drew the carmine. (Loud cheers for Paddock, who had thus won the two first events.)

9. The blow in the last round had evidently shaken Sayers, who was slow to the call of time, and came up with a suspicious mark on his potato-trap. Paddock tried to follow up his advantage, and incautiously went in, when Sayers met him with a beautiful left-hander on the snout, which sent him staggering, and put an end to his rushing for a time. This enabled Sayers to recover a little, and then, as Paddock afterwards came in, he made another call on the cheek, and got cleverly away from the return. Paddock followed him up, and heavy left-handed exchanges took place in favour of Sayers, who afterwards stopped Paddock's right

twice in succession. Good exchanges ensued to a close, and Paddock got down, just escaping Tom's right.

10. After slight, harmless exchanges they stood piping, until Paddock took the initiative, but Sayers danced under his arm, and as he turned round, pinked him on the blind goggle, and then putting in his double, renewed the home-brewed from the cheek. Paddock tried a return, but was stopped twice in succession, and then got another little 'un on the cut-water. After some neat stopping on both sides, Sayers made another call on the cheek, then on the chest, and after sharp exchanges, as Paddock rushed after him, he slipped and fell, but obviously from accident.

11. Paddock at once rushed to close quarters, but found Sayers nothing loth; they struggled for a brief period, and in the end both fell; it was obvious that Sayers was the stronger man.

12. Paddock, who was piping, and evidently fatigued, tried to lead off, but was miserably short. After a slight exchange they again closed, and after a short struggle Sayers threw and fell on his man, amidst the cheers of his admirers. One hour and two minutes had now elapsed.

13. Paddock, whose mug was all shapes but the

right, and whose remaining goggle glared most ferociously, rushed in and missed. Sayers, in getting back, fell, and there was a claim of foul; Massey and Macdonald, according to the custom of modern seconds, neglecting their man, and rushing to the referee. There was not the slightest ground for the claim, Sayers evidently having fallen from pure accident; but the usual complimentary remarks were offered by the cardsharpers and other blackguards, whose only interest was, perhaps, the value of a pot of beer depending on the result, and who were proportionately anxious to win, tie, or wrangle rather than lose their valuable (?) investments. After some time the ring-keepers succeeded in clearing these gentry away, and inducing Macdonald and Massey to return to their duty; and the referee having said 'Fight on,' the battle proceeded.

14. Paddock, to whom the delay afforded a short respite, dashed in, caught Sayers on the cheek, closed, and both fell.

15. Sayers feinted, and got on to Tom's nozzle, drawing more claret, and in getting away from a rush, crossed his legs near the stakes and fell.

16. Paddock, who was evidently getting fast worn out, at the instigation of his seconds dashed

in, as if to make a final effort to turn the scale; he let go both hands, but was short, and Sayers once more pinked him on the swollen smeller. Paddock still persevered, and more exchanges, but not of a severe description, took place, followed by a break away and a pause. Again did they get at it, and some heavy counter-hitting took place, Sayers well on the mouth and nose, and Paddock on the brow and forehead. Paddock then rushed in, and bored Sayers down at the ropes. (Another claim of foul disallowed.)

17. Paddock, desperate, rushed at once to work, and they pegged away with a will, but the punishment was all one way. At last they closed and rolled over, Sayers being top-sawyer. In the struggle and fall the spikes in Sayers' boot in some way inflicted two severe wounds in Paddock's leg, and Massey declared that the injury had been committed on purpose; but this every one who saw the fight was convinced was preposterous. Even supposing it was Sayers' spikes, it was evidently accidental, but so clumsily did they roll over that it is not impossible that it was done by the spikes in the heel of Paddock's other boot, which spikes were much longer and sharper than those of Sayers. The idea of Sayers doing such a thing

deliberately when he actually had the battle in hand is too ridiculous to admit of a question.

18. Paddock rushed in and caught Sayers on the side of the head with his right, and they closed and pegged away at close quarters until Sayers got down.

19. The in-fighting in the last round had told a tale on Paddock's nob, which was much swollen, and the left eye was now beginning to follow suit with the right. At last they got close, and both fell, Paddock under. Massey made another claim that Sayers fell with his knees on Paddock, but it was evidently an attempt to snatch a verdict.

20. Paddock tried to make an expiring effort, but was woefully short, and Sayers countered heavily with the left on the damaged cheek, then repeated the dose with great severity, staggering the burly Tom, who, however, soon collected himself, and once more led off, but out of distance. He then stood, until Sayers went up to him, popped a heavy one on the nose, and the right on the cheek, then closed at the ropes, where he fibbed Paddock very heavily, and both fell, Paddock under.

21 and last. Paddock came very slowly to the scratch, evidently without the ghost of a shadow of a chance. He was groggy, and could scarcely

see; the close quarters in the last round had done their work, and any odds might have been had on Sayers. Paddock tried a rush, but of course Sayers was nowhere near him, and as he came again, Sayers met him full on the right cheek, a very heavy hit with his left. It staggered poor Tom, who was evidently all abroad, and all but fell. He put out his hands as if to catch hold of Sayers to support himself, and the latter, who had drawn back his right hand to deliver the *coup de grâce*, seeing how matters stood, at once restrained himself, and seizing Paddock's outstretched hand, shook it warmly, and conducted him to his corner, where his seconds, seeing it was all over, at once threw up the sponge, and Sayers was proclaimed the victor in one hour and twenty minutes. Paddock was much exhausted, and it was some time before he was sufficiently himself to realize the fact that he had been defeated, when he shed bitter tears of mortification. That he had any cause for grief beyond the fact that he was defeated no one could say; indeed, if ever man persevered against nature to make a turn it was he, for notwithstanding the constant severe props he got whenever he attempted to lead, he tried it on again and again, and, to his praise be it said, took his gruel with a good temper exceeding anything we have ever witnessed on his behalf during the whole of his career. As soon as possible after the event was over the men were dressed and conveyed on board the vessel, where Paddock received every attention his state required; but it was long before he recovered from the mortification he felt at his unexpected defeat. Sayers in the meantime went round among the spectators, and made a collection for him amounting to £30."

It was said of Paddock that he was somewhat stale, and that he lacked much of the dash and power of delivery he had shown when he defeated such men as Aaron Jones, Harry Poulson, and Harry Broome, only a few years previously. Certain it is, from the account, that Sayers on this occasion altogether out-generalled his opponent by luring him, the heavier man, to do most of the running about. It is not always that a man with the "heart" and indomitable courage of Sayers also possesses the extraordinary judgment he so often displayed in his later days. In the above fight, as in his contest with Heenan (*vide* p. 86), he played to exhaust his unflinching adversary, who was then completely at his mercy.

CHAPTER VI.

GUARDING AND STOPPING.

IN the ordinary guard for the left-hand lead at the head the right arm is slightly raised with the fore-arm nearly vertical but slightly inclined towards the left so as to cause the blow to glance off. The elbow must not be stuck out, and the *arm* itself should still be as near the body as possible, for it will then be ready to drop back into the normal position to protect the mark and right side of the body. And here remember that the right arm guards the right side of the body from the *left*-hand visitations of the adversary, whilst the left arm guards the left side from his *right-handers*.

Left-hand body-blows are not so much to be feared *except on the mark*, as your right side is further away and cannot often be reached, but it is very different with the left side of your body, which

GUARD FOR LEFT-HAND LEAD AT MARK.

is open to visitations from the opponent's right. These blows, which are often very severe, coming in on the short ribs with great effect, are best guarded by dropping the left arm till it protects the whole of that side.

With the right-hand hit at the head, which is seldom used as a lead off, except where the opponent stands right leg first, you are more or less protected by your left shoulder, which often prevents the cross-counter landing on the point of the jaw; and it is important in this connection to bear in mind that the chin should not be elevated too much. Long-necked men suffer the most from right-handed blows at the head, as they naturally find difficulty in availing themselves of the sheltering protection of the shoulder. In guarding the body-blows, remember to keep the arms *close to the body*, receiving the hit as much as possible on the thick portions of the arm and fore-arm, and never attempting to guard anything on any account with the boxing-glove. It has been suggested that to guard the mark the boxing-glove should be placed over the part to be protected, but this of course is quite wrong advice, for one should never do in *boxing* anything which would be incorrect in *fighting*. The gloves are merely accessories to enable you to practise fighting without too much damage.

The five- or six-ounce gloves now used in professional contests in reality save the knuckles, and enable the hitter to continue the fight without that puffiness of the knuckles which, in the old days, resulted from repeatedly coming in contact with the harder portion of the adversary's head, and which rendered the hitting, at the close of many contests, quite ineffective. On such occasions, as in the case of the Sayers and Heenan fight, the blows at last became mere pushes, and were, as far as the bigger man's hits were concerned, very soft on account of the state of his knuckles. Sayers retained his left hand alone, but was too exhausted to do much with it, whilst Heenan was practically blind.

Perhaps the best general advice with regard to defence is to use guards almost exclusively for the body, and trust to slipping, getting out of reach, ducking, and the side step for protecting the head. Still, head-guard with both hands should frequently be practised; and never lose sight of the fact that with the elbows well in and the fore-arms only slightly inclined from the perpendicular, you cause the hits to slide off without any shock to yourself.

GUARD FOR LEFT-HAND LEAD AT HEAD.

The advantage of this method is particularly felt when you are opposed to a heavy, strong man who habitually chops heavily down on to your guard.

Again, if you raise the elbow unduly you are at once at a mechanical disadvantage, for, in that position, your fore-arm is very apt to be hit into your face, and you will then probably suffer more than if you had taken the hit of the boxing-glove full in the face.

Always chance taking a flush hit in the face in preference to a severe body-blow, *i. e.* in the matter of *guarding* proper let it be for the benefit of the body chiefly, and trust more to *avoiding* when the head is threatened.

These remarks are particularly applicable to small and middle-sized men, who, when opposed to heavy metal, have to do most of the running about. Very big men usually should pay great attention to guarding body-blows, and should rely on a straight left and steady right to keep their shorter opponents at a distance.

In February 1857, two very noteworthy fights took place between the gallant Tom Sayers and Aaron Jones, who was not only a much bigger man, but a plucky and skilful fighter. They are very good samples of what prize-fights *ought* to be—

K

plenty of science, great exhibition of endurance, and fairness throughout. It must be remembered that Aaron Jones had given such a very powerful and resolute customer as Tom Paddock enough to do, and that he and his supporters expected to gain a fairly easy victory over a middle weight of Tom Sayers' calibre. The result speaks volumes in favour of Tom's generalship, and his stopping and hitting powers.

TOM SAYERS v. AARON JONES.

"*Round* 1. On baring their fore-quarters to the piercing breeze, a perceptible shiver ran through the carcases of the combatants. Sayers looked in perfect condition; every muscle was perceptible, and we doubt whether there was an ounce of superfluous flesh about him. There was a smile of confidence on his lips and bright sparkle in his eye that betokened extraordinary health and spirits. His attitude was artistic and firm, yet light. Of course he stood on the defensive, and eyed his heavier opponent. There did not appear to be that disparity of size that really existed, for Jones stooped rather on throwing himself on guard, and thus reduced his height almost to a level with that of the gallant Tom, who was upright as a dart. Aaron's condition did not seem to us so first-rate as the first glance at him had led us to suppose. His muscles, though large, were too well covered, while his back and chest also displayed much superfluous meat, and we should say that his weight could not have been less than 12st. 4lbs. He, like Sayers, looked confident, but was far more serious in his demeanour. They both commenced the round with the utmost caution, sparring, and attempting to draw one another into something like an opening; but for a long time neither would throw a chance away. At length Jones dashed out left and right; but the blows passed over Tom's shoulders, and Tom with quickness tapped Aaron on the face, but without force. Sayers now let go his left, but Jones retreated. Tom persevered, and was cleverly stopped. In a third attempt, after more dodging, he got heavily on Aaron's mouth and stepped back without a return. Jones now assumed the offensive, but was stopped, and Tom, after another dodge or two, planted his left heavily on the mark, and then the same hand on the side of Aaron's nut, but not heavily. Jones returned heavily on the right peeper, and shortly after made a second call at the same establishment.

More stopping and dodging, until Sayers paid another visit to Aaron's kisser, Jones missing his return. Each now stopped a lead; but immediately after Jones popped in his left on the snuff-box, a heavy hit without a return. Tom grinned a ghastly grin; but the crack evidently made him see stars. Jones attempted to repeat the dose; but Tom got well away, and, as he retreated, popped his left on the neck. More excellent stopping on both sides, and, after a few harmless exchanges, Tom tried a double with his left and got on the throat, but the blow lacked steam. Jones returned with quickness over the left peeper, inflicting a cut and drawing the claret. ('First blood' for Jones.) Tom, although staggered, was undaunted, and went at his man with determination. He once more got on the bread-basket heavily. Good counter-hits followed, in which Jones again reached Tom's damaged peeper, drawing more of the essential, and Tom delivered a straight one on the snout, removing a small portion of the bark. Tom then got on the left eye, and, after some sharp punching at close quarters, both fell. This round lasted exactly half-an-hour.

2. Tom came up much flushed, and the crimson distilling from his damaged eye. After a little

dodging, he tried his double, but did not get it home. He tried a second time, but was stopped, and Jones returned on the left eye. This led to very heavy counters, each on the larboard goggle. Jones now feinted, and popped his left on the nose. They got hold of one another, swung round, broke away, and Sayers then popped his left again on the left eye. Severe exchanges followed at close quarters, and both in the end were down.

3. Sayers quickly led off with his left, and was stopped. He then tried his double, but was short. In a third essay he got home on Aaron's nose, but not heavily. Twice again did he pop in gentle taps, but he now napped another rattler on the left eye. Severe exchanges followed, Aaron again turning on the stream from Tom's left brow, and Tom tapping his opponent's snuff-box. More exchanges in favour of Jones, and in the end both fell in a scrambling struggle, Jones under.

4. Tom's left brow and the left side of his canister were much swollen, but he was still confident, and led off, Jones countering him well on the mouth. Heavy exchanges followed, Tom on the nose, and Jones on the left cheek, and both again slipped down, the ground being anything but level.

5. Tom let fly his left, but was neatly stopped; Jones returned on the side of the brain-pan, and got down.

6. Sayers came up, looking very serious, and it subsequently turned out that he was suffering from severe cramp in the stomach and lower extremities. He went in, feinted, and got well home on Jones's left eye. This led to sharp exchanges and a close, when both were down, Jones being underneath. Aaron had now a bump on his left peeper, which was apparently closing.

7. Aaron lost no time in sending out his left, which fell on Tom's chest. Heavy counter-hits followed, Jones on the nose, and Tom on the mouth. More exchanges in favour of Sayers, who again got on Aaron's damaged optic, and the latter got down.

8. Sayers went to his man, and tried his double, the second blow dropping on Aaron's sneezer, and Tom then got cleverly away from the return. Exchanges ensued, Tom on the mark, and Aaron on the mazzard; Aaron then got home his right heavily on the left side of Tom's knowledge-box, then his left on the left eye, and in the close Sayers was down.

9. Aaron led off, but was well stopped, and this

led to some sharp exchanges, Jones on the bad peeper, and Tom on the left brow. Sayers tried another double, and once more visited Aaron's nose, but not heavily. More mutual stopping, and Jones, at length, in getting away, slipped and fell. One hour had now elapsed.

10. Tom planted his left on the beak, and received a little one in return on the forehead. Jones now let fly his left and right, but was cleverly stopped. In a second essay he got home on the left cheek. Heavy exchanges followed, Tom getting on both peepers, and Jones on the side of Tom's cranium with both daddles, and Tom fell.

11. Aaron had now a mark on each peeper, the left fast closing. Tom's left, too, appeared almost shut up. Jones tried to take the lead, but missed; Sayers likewise missed his return. Exchanges followed in favour of Jones, who, in the end, closed, and in the struggle both fell, Jones uppermost.

12. No time lost; both quickly at it, and some sharp exchanges took place in favour of Jones, who got heavily on Tom's nose. Tom made his left on the body heavily, and they then pegged away wildly at close quarters until Jones got down.

13. Aaron dashed in and pegged away left and

right, but without precision, and ultimately bored his man down.

14. Jones feinted, and popped his left on the left eye, without a return. Tom then let go his left, but was short, and Jones, in dashing at him in return, slipped and fell.

15. Aaron led off, left and right, but Tom got away. He came again, and tried to plant his left, but was short. He then tried his double, but Jones got away. Both now sparred and dodged, but nothing came of it. At last Jones dashed in, and heavy exchanges took place in favour of Jones, who, however, in the end, fell.

16. Both at once went to work, and heavy exchanges took place, each napping it on the left ogle, and both fell through the ropes.

17. Tom's forehead and left eye much disfigured. Jones let fly his left and right on the sides of the nob very heavily, and both again fell through the ropes.

18. Tom came up slowly, and was nailed on the damaged peeper. In return he caught Aaron on the brow, but not heavily. Jones then made his left and right on the side of the head and left eye, and Tom retaliated on the nose a little one. A close followed, and in the end both were down, Jones under.

19. Tom dodged, and got home on Aaron's smeller with his left, and Aaron then made both hands on the left side of Tom's wig-block. A close and sharp struggle, when both fell, Tom under.

20. Jones dashed in, and ¡let go both hands on the head. Tom returned on the left brow, and both fell backwards.

21. Aaron again dashed in. He missed his right, closed, and both fell, Jones under.

22. Tom now led off, but missed, and Jones caught him heavily with his right on the frontispiece, and knocked him down. ('First knock-down' for Jones.)

23. Tom, on coming up, showed the effect of the last blow on his forehead. He attempted to lead off, but was very short. He tried again with a like result; and Jones, in letting go both hands in return, over-reached himself and fell.

24. Aaron rattled in, planted his left and right on the scent-box and left ear, the latter very heavy, and bored Tom down.

25. Tom came up bleeding from a severe cut on the left lug, and his gnomon much out of straight. He tried to lead off, but Jones caught him on the right brow, but not very heavily. Tom then got

home on the body, and tremendous counter-hits followed in favour of Jones, who, in the end, slipped and fell, Tom catching him, just as he reached the ground, on the side of the head.

26. Jones went in left and right, closed, and both were down. Sayers was now very weak, and the Jonesites were in ecstasies.

27. Aaron led off, getting well on the side of Tom's nut with his right. Tom missed his return, and Jones then planted his left and right on the top of the skull; closed at the ropes, where Tom managed to throw him, but not heavily.

28. Jones led off, and got well on Tom's nose with his left, and Tom returned on the side of the head. After a little dodging, Jones popped his left on Tom's left peeper, and his right on the jaw, again flooring Tom and falling on him.

29. Tom, who was excessively weak, came up slowly, but determined; he tried his left at the body, but was short. Jones then let fly his left in return, but was countered on the mouth. He then planted his left and right on Tom's damaged listener, and in the end fell.

30. Aaron, after a few dodges, once more popped a little 'un on Tom's ear. Tom thereupon dashed in, but got a little one on the nose, and another on

the side of the head, and Jones, in getting away, fell, laughing.

31. Jones attempted to lead off, but Tom got away. Jones followed him up, caught him again on the side of the nob, closed, and both rolled over together.

32. Jones dashed in, and planted both hands on the brain-pan, closed, and forced Tom down.

33. Jones again rushed in, but inflicted no damage, and again bored Tom down.

34. Jones still forced the fighting, and caught Tom, who seemed very tired, on the side of the head, and in the end both slipped down.

35. Sayers was forced down, after getting a gentle reminder on the side of his damaged figure-head.

36. Tom, a little refreshed, sparred about for wind, until Jones went in, and heavy exchanges took place in favour of Jones, when both fell backwards.

37. Tom, recovering a little, tried his double, but Jones got away, and, as Tom came, he nailed him on the left brow. Tom then made his left on the mark, but again napped it heavily on the left eye. Aaron now got on the nose with his left—a heavy spank—and, in getting back, he staggered and fell.

38. Jones dodged, and planted his left on the mouth heavily, and his right on the side of the head. Tom returned slightly on the nose, and, after slight exchanges, both fell.

39. Very slight exchanges, and Sayers slipped down.

40. After a little sparring they got close, and exchanges took place, each getting it on the mouth. Sayers then tried his left at the mark, but Jones got away. Tom followed him up, and was caught by Aaron, left and right, on the side of the head and fell.

41. Tom came up, shook himself and rattled in, but he got it on the top of his cranium. Jones, in stepping back, fell. Two hours had now expired.

42. Jones, steady, let go his left on the side of Tom's head, and then both mauleys on the same spot. Tom followed him up, but got it again on the brow. He, however, got home on Jones's body, and in retreating slipped and fell.

43. Long sparring for wind, until Jones once more made play on the left side of Tom's occiput, and then on his snout. Tom returned on the latter organ again, but not heavily. He now tried his favourite double, but did not get home. In a second attempt he got heavily on Aaron's pro-

boscis, and got away. Exchanges followed, in which Tom again delivered heavily on the nose with his left, and in the end Jones dropped.

44. Tom was now evidently recovering from his exhaustion. He came up steadier, and sparred shiftily until Jones commenced the attack, when he stopped him neatly. Heavy counter-hits followed on the jaw, after which Sayers tried the double once again, but was stopped. More good counter-hits, Tom getting well on Aaron's left eye, and receiving on the mouth. Aaron's left eye all but closed.

45. More sparring, until Jones let fly his left, but Sayers got away. Exchanges followed, Tom on the whistler, and Jones on the nose, but not heavily. More sharp counter-hitting, Tom once more getting on the left eye severely. Jones returned, but not effectively, with both hands on the side of the head, and in getting away from the return he fell.

46. Jones succeeded in planting a spanking hit from the left on the left eye, and then another with the same hand on the left cheek. In a third attempt he was stopped. Heavy counter-hits followed, and in the end Jones fell, Sayers falling over him.

47. Aaron feinted with his left, and got well on Tom's nose; a very straight hit. Tom in return tried his double, but was short. After some more ineffectual attempts they got to it, and tremendous exchanges took place, each getting it on the nose and left eye, and in the end Jones got down. Two hours, fifteen minutes.

48. Tom tried to lead off, but was stopped, and Jones planted his left on the cheek. Tom now stopped two of Jones's hits, after which heavy exchanges took place, Tom getting well on to the left eye, and Jones on the nose. More sharp exchanges, left and right, each getting pepper in earnest, and favours mutually divided. A break away, and to it again, ding-dong, and Tom drew the crimson from Aaron's left peeper, which was now effectually closed. In the end Jones fell. It was now anybody's battle; Tom had quite recovered his wind, and was nearly as strong as his heavier opponent.

49. Both much punished. Sayers sparred until Jones tried to lead off, when he got away. Jones followed him up, but was short in his deliveries. In the end they closed, and as they were falling Tom popped his right sharply on Aaron's back.

50. Jones, after sparring, led off, and got home on the nose, but not heavily; Tom returned on

the right peeper, and some pretty exchanges left and right took place, followed by a break away, and Jones then stopped Tom's left; Tom, in return, stopped Aaron, and planted his left on the mark, and then on the left eye, and Jones got down.

51. Jones led off, but was stopped. He persevered, and a good give-and-take rally followed, Jones getting on the left eye, and Tom on the left cheek heavily. Tom next got on the mouth, drawing the Burgundy, and then on the nose and left cheek. Another sharp rally followed, after a break away, and in the end both down.

52. Sayers visibly improving, while Jones fell off. Jones was short in his lead, and Tom returned on the smelling-bottle, and got away. Jones followed, and dashed out his left, but Tom ducked his head. Tom then got home on the mouth and nose, and drew more of the ruby from the latter ornament. Jones succeeded in returning a little 'un on the left eye, and Sayers slipped down.

53. Jones, who was bleeding from the left eye and mouth, led off, but was well stopped. He then missed his left, but in the end heavy exchanges left and right took place, Jones on the side of the nut and the neck, and in getting back he fell.

54. Tom now essayed a lead, but was stopped. A second attempt reached Aaron's body, but not heavily, and Jones returned on the nose. Tom tried his double, but missed, and Jones popped a little one on the mouth, and then his left on the left eye, and fell in the corner.

55. Tom dodged about until he got within distance, and then got home heavily on the mark. Jones returned on the jaw with his right, but not heavily. After some more sparring, Jones dashed in, when Tom met him very sharply on the right cheek-bone with his left, and Aaron fell all of a heap. He was carried to his corner, where it was with the utmost difficulty he could be got round at the call of 'Time.'

56. Jones came up all abroad, and Tom popped in another spank on the same spot, whereupon Jones again fell. It was thought to be all over; but, by dint of shaking him up, Aaron was again enabled to respond to the call.

57. Tom rushed at his man to administer the *coup de grâce*, but going in without precision, he contrived to run against Aaron's left, which was swung wildly out, and the blow, which alighted on Tom's nose, regularly staggered him. He quickly recovered himself, and went in again, but Jones

fell weak. After this, the battle continued to the 62nd round, Jones getting gradually blind, and Sayers becoming very tired. At length in the 62nd round, after slight exchanges, the men, who were much exhausted, stood still, looking at each other for some time, their seconds covering them with rugs. Upon this the referee and umpires called on them to go in and finish. Both went to the scratch, but on Sayers approaching Jones, the latter retreated to his corner, and Tom, in obedience to the orders of his seconds, declined going to fight him there. It was getting dark, and it was clear that Jones and his friends were determined not to throw a chance away. The referee once more called on Jones to go to the scratch, which he did, but with precisely the same result; and the referee, seeing that Tom was not strong enough to go with prudence to finish on his adversary's ground, and that Jones was unwilling to try the question at the scratch in his then exhausted state, ordered the men to shake hands, leaving the motion as to further hostilities to a future day. Both were severely punished; each had a peeper closed; Jones's right was fast following his left, and his right hand was injured; so that a second meeting the same week was not to be thought of. The fight lasted exactly three hours. The men and their friends now hastened to regain the vessel, and it was dark long ere the last of the company were safely on board. Of course there were many laughable accidents in the mud, through which all had to wade; but luckily, nothing occurred of a serious nature to mar the pleasures of the day, which, although in some measure clouded by the fact that the battle was not finished, still left sufficient impression on the minds of the spectators to cause them to remember this brilliant passage of arms, which formed so hopeful an opening to the pugilistic year 1857. The vessel conveyed the company with all due speed to a convenient place for debarkation, whence they obtained a passage by railway to the Metropolis, which was reached in safety by nine o'clock. Numerous complaints were made by the disappointed ones who went to the Great Northern Railway, at the manner in which they were deceived; and the only consolation is that we are sorry for those whom we should have been glad to welcome at the ring-side, but who have themselves alone to blame for not finding out the final fixture as many others had done; while as to others of a certain class, who are always more free than welcome, we can with truth say their room was better than their company; and we rejoice, with others who were present, that they were so completely sold. Some unlucky wights got a sort of hint as to the fixture, and arrived within a few miles of the spot, at a late hour in the afternoon, and were landed, but unluckily for them, on the wrong island, and here the poor fellows had to remain all night, and sleep under a haystack. The boats that landed them had departed, and they could make no one hear; so that, cold, hungry, and thirsty, they had to weather the cold severe night in the best way they could."

The renewed battle, fixed for February 10, 1857, took place on the banks of the Medway, on the same spot as the former gallant encounter.

SAYERS *v.* AARON JONES.

"*Round* 1. On toeing the scratch the condition of both men struck the spectators with admiration. In our opinion it was perfect on both sides, but the development of muscle was decidedly in favour of Sayers, who is better ribbed up, and has his thews and sinews laid on in the right place. He looked brown, wiry, and healthy, and for a middle weight, seemed wonderfully big. Jones, who is of fairer complexion, was altogether more delicate in appearance than Sayers, and although so much taller, heavier, and longer, did not loom out so much larger as might be expected. He is a fine-made, muscular young fellow, but still there is an appearance about him which at once leads to the conclusion that his stamina is scarcely fitted for the wear and tear of gladiatorial encounters. He is about 26 years of age, and in height is over 5ft. 11in., while Tom Sayers is 31, and is little more than 5ft. 8in. It was soon seen that Sayers intended to pursue different tactics to those he adopted on the previous occasion. He dodged about for a few seconds, and then let go his left and right with great quickness, but Jones stopped him neatly, and in getting back fell.

2. Tom came up smiling, feinted with his left, and then tried his favourite double; the first hit was stopped, but the second caught Aaron on the chin. This he repeated, and got away without a return. After trying his double once more without success, he planted his left very heavily on the mark. Jones at once went to close quarters, and some quick in-fighting took place in favour of Sayers, who got well on to Aaron's snuff-box with

his left, drawing 'first blood.' Jones got on the left side of Tom's head, but not heavily, and at length both fell.

3. Both quick to the call of 'Time,' and Sayers at once went to work with his left, Jones countering him heavily, each getting it on the forehead. Tom then popped his left on the mark, and Aaron returned, but not heavily, on the nose. Tom now again planted the left on the mark, and was stopped in a second effort. Heavy exchanges next took place, Tom once more drawing the cork from a cut on Aaron's sniffer, and receiving on the left ear. After a few dodges, Tom again approached, and made a heavy call on Aaron's bread-basket, then planted a stinger between the eyes, and got away laughing. He attempted to repeat the dose, but was stopped. Another effort was more successful, and he dropped on the mark, staggering Jones, who, however, recovered himself, and popped his left on the chest, then on the left cheek, but not heavily. Sparring until Tom got within distance, and shot out his left heavily on the proboscis, without a return, Jones being a little wild. Tom now essayed his double, but Jones got away, and returned on the mouth. Tom persevered, and napped a little 'un on the

left eye for his pains; still he would be at work,
and got well on Aaron's left peeper, drawing the
ruby. Heavy exchanges followed, Jones getting
on Tom's left brow, and Tom turning on the
home-brewed from Aaron's nasal organ. After
two or three slight exchanges in favour of Sayers,
he again put the double on, reaching the left cheek
and bread-basket. Next he popped another hot
one on the victualling department, receiving a
slight return on the forehead. After a break
away he stole in, and bang went his left on Aaron's
damaged eye, drawing more of the ruby. A
merry little rally followed in favour of Sayers,
who at last broke away, and sparred as if blown
from his fast fighting. Jones approached to take
advantage of this, when Tom propped him on the
brow, and then on the forehead. Jones returned
with both hands, but not heavily, on the brow and
body, and another bustling rally came off, Tom
getting home on the left ogle and throat heavily,
and Aaron on the larboard cheek. Another break
away, and Tom, on getting himself together,
resumed the double, got on the mark very heavily,
and then popped his right on the left side of
Aaron's nob. He got away laughing, and as
Jones tried to follow him up he warned him off by

a pop on the left eye. A heavy rally at last took place, in which Jones got sharply on the left ear, and Sayers on the left eye, and this protracted and well-fought round was concluded by Tom slipping down.

4. Sayers on coming up, showed a mark on his forehead, and another on his left ear, while Aaron's left eye and nose were much out of the perpendicular. Tom lost no time in going to work, and planted his one, two: the left on Aaron's right eye, and the right on the left jaw, knocking Aaron off his pins. ('First knock down' for Sayers.) Jones seemed all abroad, and it was with the greatest difficulty that he was got round to the call of 'Time.'

5. Sayers at once went in left and right, but he was too anxious to finish his handiwork, and the blows lacked precision. He reached the side of Aaron's nob, and Jones returned slightly on the same spot, and after mild exchanges both fell. This gave Jones time to get round, and by the commencement of the next round, he had shaken off the nasty one he had got in the fourth.

6. Tom tried his double, but missed, and Jones rushed in to close, when Tom caught him round the neck, and punched him heavily on the left

peeper and nozzle, drawing more of the ruby. In the end both fell, Sayers under.

7. Aaron came up with his left eye all but closed. Tom let go his left, but Jones returned on the nose. Tom tried again, and got on the ribs; Jones returned merrily left and right, but did little damage, and Tom fell in his corner.

8. Jones dashed in and pegged away with both mauleys on the left side of Tom's knowledge-box; Tom returned on the left brow and closed, when both fell, Tom under.

9. Jones again dashed in, and some sharp infighting took place, followed by a close, in which both fell, Jones, this time, being underneath.

10. Tom's dial seemed flushed, but his eyes were still uninjured. Jones rattled in to close, some quick fibbing took place, followed by a long struggle for the fall, which Sayers got, and fell on his man. In drawing his legs away, he brought one foot in smart contact with Aaron's leg, which was claimed as a foul kick, but disallowed by the referee, being evidently accidental.

11. Jones again took the initiative, and let go both hands on Tom's forehead, and then his left on the nose. Tom returned on the left eye, and then a squasher on the mark. Exchanges,

and Sayers fell, evidently fatigued by his fast fighting.

12. Jones persevered in his forcing system, and got on the left side of Tom's cranium, Tom returning very heavily on the nose. Jones again went in, and planted his left under the left optic, closed, and both fell, Tom under.

13. Jones rushed at Tom, and pegged away at him in his corner. It was a rambling, scrambling round, and both fell, no mischief being done.

14. Jones again led off, but Tom popped him well on the left eye, and Aaron fell on his face.

15. Good exchanges on the left cheek, after which Jones got well on Tom's throat, closed, and both were down.

16. Jones dashed at Tom, popped in his left and right on the frontispiece and nose, and bored Tom through the ropes.

17. Jones again opened the ball, got on to Tom's left ear, closed, and both were down.

18. Aaron led off on Tom's nose; Tom returned on the left eye, very heavily, and Aaron fell.

19. Tom resumed the initiative, and reached Aaron's nose,—by his favourite double. Jones returned, but not heavily, on the forehead, after which Tom cross-countered him prettily on the

left peeper, and this led to exchanges in favour of Jones, when Sayers fell.

20. Both quick to work; good exchanges, and in the end Jones floored Tom by a heavy right-hander on the jaw. (Loud cheers for Jones.)

21. Jones elated rushed in, but Tom steadied him by a straight 'un on the left cheek, and Jones dropped.

22. Aaron missed both hands, and after some sparring Tom caught him heavily on the left ogle, and Jones dropped. Sayers also fell.

23. Tom, who seemed getting fresh wind, rattled in, and planted his double on the nose and mouth. Jones rushed at him, and in the scramble Sayers was bored over.

24. Tom popped a left-hander on the 'grubbery,' received a little one on the nose, and fell.

25. Heavy exchanges, Sayers on the left eye, and Aaron on the nose. Jones slipped down.

26. Jones led off with both hands, but not heavily, and Tom returned severely on the nose and left eye, which was now quite closed. Jones fell.

27. Jones rushed to close quarters, and after a brief struggle fell.

28. Tom feinted, and popped his left twice on

Aaron's damaged peeper. Jones returned on the nose, and Tom fell.

29. Jones went to work, catching Tom over the right eye, and Sayers, in getting back, fell.

30. Both went to work with good will, and after sharp exchanges in favour of Sayers, Jones got down.

31. Aaron tried to lead off, but was well stopped, and Tom returned on the mark. He next popped his left on the left cheek, and in getting away slipped down, just escaping a heavy upper-cut.

32. Tom feinted, and then got well on to Aaron's nose with his left, and retreated, Aaron pursuing him. At length they got close, and Tom sent in a stiffener on the scent-box, receiving a right-hander on the left ear, which opened a cut received in their former fight, and both fell.

33. Tom again seemed tired, and sparred for wind. Jones came to him, when Tom let go his left on the jaw, closed, and both fell.

34. Tom slowest to time. He tried his left, but was stopped; Aaron closed, and Tom fibbed him on the left eye as they fell.

35. After a little dodging, they got close, and heavy counters were exchanged. They now closed, and, as they fell, Tom again put a little one on Aaron's left eye.

36. A close and a struggle, when both fell, Jones under.

37. Sayers led off, but was stopped, and after a wild scramble, Tom fell. One hour and five minutes had now elapsed.

38. Jones dashed in, but Tom steadied him by a left-hander on the left cheek, and Aaron got down.

39. Jones, still first, let go left and right on the mouth and the left cheek. Sayers returned on the blind eye, and got down.

40. Jones let fly his left, but missed. Slight exchanges to a close, and both down.

41. Jones, on the forcing system, planted his left on the jaw and then on the left ear, and as he was pursuing his man he fell on his face.

42. Jones missed his left. Tom returned openhanded on the back, and Jones dropped.

43. Jones dashed to a close at the ropes, where they pegged away smartly but ineffectually until they fell.

44. Tom got home on the left jaw. Aaron missed both hands and fell.

45. Jones went to work, but without precision, and as Sayers retreated, Jones fell on his face. It was clear that Tom was carefully nursing himself, while Jones, feeling that both his ogles were going,

was forcing the fighting, in order to tire out his opponent before he became blind.

46. Jones rattled in and caught Tom on the left cheek, but not heavily. Tom returned on the left peeper, drawing more claret, and Jones dropped.

47. Aaron, in his anxiety, missed both mauleys, and Tom caught him a heavy right-hander on the proboscis, whereupon Jones dropped.

48. Jones went to his man, who nailed him on the left ogle, and, as Jones persevered, he caught him heavily on the throat, and Jones fell.

49. Tom tried to lead off, but was short, and Jones returned heavily on the ribs with his right. He then attempted to close, but, on Sayers catching hold of him, he fell.

50. Tom tried his double, but Jones stopped him, and in getting away slipped down.

51. Slight exchanges; Jones on the mouth and Sayers on the nose, and Jones down.

52. Jones led off and was neatly stopped. Tom missed his return, and Jones fell forward.

53. Tom led off and got on Aaron's blind eye,— Jones returned very slightly on the nose, and fell.

54. Tom planted his left heavily on the mark, which led to mutual exchanges, and Jones fell.

55. Tom feinted and popped both hands slightly

on Aaron's good eye, which began to tell tales. Jones returned on the left ear, but it was too long a shot to do damage, and Sayers fell.

56. Aaron opened the ball, and planted his left and right on the nose and ear twice in succession. He then rushed in, when Tom stopped him by a straight one on the blind eye, and Jones fell.

57. Jones again went to work, but Tom was too quick on his pins, and got out of harm's way. Sayers missed his return, and Jones fell.

58. Tom, still on the nursing system, kept himself quiet, waiting for the attack. Jones went in, but Tom stepped back; slight exchanges ensued, and Jones fell.

59. Jones let go his left; Tom ducked his nut, and the blow went over, when Jones fell. A claim of foul, as Jones fell without a blow. The referee said, 'Fight on.'

60. Jones popped his left on the chest; Tom returned on the left cheek, and Jones fell. One hour and a half had now elapsed.

61. Jones, still first to begin, got on Tom's nose and fell, Tom falling over him.

62. Jones planted his left very slightly on the side of Tom's nob; Tom just touched him on the smeller in return, and Jones down again.

63. Jones rushed in, caught Tom on the chin, and Tom fell. The blow was not very heavy.

64. Jones missed both hands, got a little one on the side of his nut, and fell.

65. Jones got home left and right, heavily on the ribs; Tom retaliated on the mark, and Jones down.

66. Jones let go his left, but Tom avoided the force of the blow by stepping back. He returned on the neck, and Jones got down.

67—71. In all these rounds Jones led off, but did no mischief, from Tom's quickness on his pins, and in each Jones was down.

72. Tom still waiting and resting himself; Jones came in and planted his right on the ribs. Tom returned on the right ogle, but not heavily, and Jones down, his right eye going fast. Sayers, though much tired, had both eyes well open, and his face presented no very serious marks of punishment.

73. Heavy exchanges, and Jones fell on his face.

74. Jones tried to lead off, but was stopped. Counter-hits, Sayers on the nose, and Jones on the cheek, and Jones fell.

75. Heavy exchanges in favour of Sayers, and Jones down.

76. Jones, who saw he must do it quickly or not at all, dashed in recklessly, but was stopped. Tom popped a little one on the nose, and Jones down.

77. Jones was again stopped, and Tom got well on his good eye, and Jones fell.

78. Sayers stopped Aaron's rush, and again got on to his good peeper. Jones instantly fell on his knees.

79. Aaron delivered his left on the nose, and in trying to repeat it fell on his face. Another claim that he had fallen without a blow not allowed.

80. Heavy exchanges, Tom getting again on Aaron's good peeper, which was now all but shut up, and Jones down.

81. Jones led off, but woefully out of distance, and fell forward.

82. Exchanges in favour of Sayers, and Jones down weak.

83. Tom, who saw his time had arrived, went in, planted his favourite double on Aaron's good peeper, and Jones fell.

84. After a little fiddling, Tom crept close again, dashed out his left on the good eye, and then on the cheek, and Jones down.

85—and last. Jones made a last effort, was easily

stopped, and as he turned round Tom caught him on his right a terrific half-arm hit on the right eye, and knocked him off his pins. It was evidently a finisher. Poor Aaron's nob fell forward, and it was at once apparent that his remaining daylight was closed; and his seconds, seeing this, of course threw up the sponge, Tom being proclaimed the winner, after a gallant battle of exactly two hours. Sayers at once went to shake hands with his brave antagonist, and then repaired on board the vessel, whither he was soon followed by Jones, whose damaged peeper was at once looked to by a medical friend. The poor fellow was very severely punished, but he did not seem to feel this so acutely as he did the bitter disappointment of having to play second fiddle to one so much smaller than himself. The expedition quickly got under way, and all reached the Metropolis by nine o'clock. As soon as Sayers was dressed he went round among his fellow-passengers, and made a collection for his fallen antagonist, which reached the sum of £8. Beyond fatigue and a few trifling bruises on his forehead and nose, he was unscathed, and he certainly could scarcely be said to have a black eye."

CHAPTER VII.

THE 'SIDE-STEP' AND 'SLIPPING.'

IN the chapter on Timing and Countering the value of making your "stop"—for as such your counter should be regarded—also serve as an attack, or have an attacking effect, is enlarged upon. Here also the object is to altogether avoid the attack of your opponent without what is technically known as guarding proper. Say your adversary leads at your head with his left, and you have decided not to counter or cross-counter him; step smartly to the right with your right foot, not too far, and at the same time duck and hit at his mark with your left.

This is a particularly desirable defence when opposed to a bigger man, and, having myself usually boxed up-hill, *i.e.* with heavier men, I may be somewhat prejudiced in its favour, so do not let these remarks carry undue weight.

THE SIDE-STEP.

It would, for instance, be extremely unadvisable for the taller man to do much ducking and avoiding, as he would only bring his head into closer proximity to his adversary's fist. He should not ever diminish his height, but try to maintain his reach and fight his man *at a distance*. Short strong men, "sturdy varlets" like our old friend Bat Mullins, always try to get into the half-arm work, as it is almost sure to pay them better, though in Bat's case, it must be said that he is about the longest-armed man in England for his inches, and can hit as far as many a six-footer.

Then there is this advantage in the side-step: it does not throw you much out of your bearings, but the opponent has to make a half-turn round to the left in order to again face you.

"Slipping" is another way of avoiding punishment, and it is own brother, or at least first cousin, to the side-step, only it is a more complete get-out-of-the-way defence, and reminds one of the clown in the circus who slips away and then pops up again in an unexpected place with "Here we are again."

It may be necessary, on occasions, to get quite clear of further complications, and by this manœuvre you almost run away, but you should do so sideways, like a crab, only quicker, and never altogether turn your back to the enemy, who should be kept at any rate in the corner of your eye. He may come round too rapidly, and if you can avoid his upper-cut there may be a good chance at his ribs with your right.

In all steps aside or retreats you should be careful not to do more than you need to serve the purpose. Every scrap of over-exertion or needless strain may be so much off your store of strength or activity in a close finish. You want to keep a little in hand for a "push," and remember that, though continued attacking is the most fatiguing, unnecessary running about is almost as much so, and may reduce you to a condition of weakness when the critical moment arrives.

Be careful never to cross the legs; the foot which is nearest the point towards which you are advancing or retreating should be the one to move first.

Avoid anything approaching a shambling, shuffling mode of getting about, for this is particularly likely to get you into difficulties if the ring is on turf or on ground which is at all uneven.

Occasionally when your retreat has been just sufficient to serve its purpose, and when the adversary *believes* you are still well on the retreat, you may gain a point by immediately bringing up the retreating foot a few inches—in this way you will be a shade nearer your opponent than he thinks, and may be able to reach him sooner.

Both the side-step and slipping may be brought into play if your adversary stands right foot foremost, only the movements will be made to your left instead of to the right; and remember that in boxing with such an opponent your right hand will be far more brought into play; also bear in mind that he has seen lots of men box like you, but you have probably come across very few who box right foot first. (*Vide* Chapter X. on Right-handed Boxers.)

In all manœuvres try as far as possible to maintain the *relative position of the feet*. Depend upon it, it is only by constantly bearing this in mind that one can hope to even approximate to really first-rate leg work. Every movement should be neat, quick, and decided—not shambling like the gait of a bear in a hurry to pick up a penny bun.

The advantage of avoiding heavy hits *early in a fight* with a more powerful man is obvious: very often when many rounds have been fought it will be found easier to use other stops, because the adversary will have probably become weaker and *slower*, but in the early stages great caution should be observed. It is possible, though by no means certain, that Corbett would not have defeated J. L. Sullivan had he not used the side-step in Round 3 when the Champion was fresh and dangerous.

In going through the following account it will be noticed how well Corbett realized the necessity of feeling his way and biding his time in dealing with such a powerful administerer of knock-out blows as the redoubtable " J. L."

How that plucky and determined middle-weight fighter Bob Fitzsimmons in his turn defeated Corbett will be found in Chapter V.

CORBETT *v.* SULLIVAN.

The fight was decided in the Olympic Club, New Orleans, La., on September 7, 1892. About 10,000 spectators witnessed it. Betting was 4 to 1 on Sullivan.

The following is the fight by rounds—

"*Round* 1. Both men were smiling. Sullivan rushed in, but missed a left-hand lead, Corbett cleverly retreating. The Californian parried a thrust and retreated once more. His activity was

THE 'SIDE-STEP' AND 'SLIPPING.' 183

remarkable, and the first minute was spent in harmless sparring. The crowd began to hiss Corbett, and he continued his retreating tactics until half the round was over. Sullivan frowned, and seemed angry as the gong struck. Not an effective blow was struck during the round.

2. The men sparred at long range for almost a minute, Corbett dodging away every time the Champion attempted to force matters. He ducked a left-hand lead cleverly, but the big fellow rushed him to the ropes. Fierce fighting followed. Sullivan landed twice on Corbett's face, followed by an upper-cut. Then Jem was even wilder than ever, flying about the arena like a hunted deer. Sullivan watched his chance, and got in a left-hand swing, but it did not land with full force, Corbett getting back with a light punch in the belly.

3. Sullivan missed an excellent chance, and bit his lips reproachfully. Corbett made a beautiful side-step and evaded a right-hand lead at his stomach; it was evident to all that he was going to make a long fight of it. John rushed in and landed lightly on the back, but it was only a glancing blow. Jem came nearer, and got in a rib-roaster on Sullivan's heart. Sullivan's return was short, and did no damage. Corbett landed two left-hand

swings on the Champion's jaw, and for the first time in the fight did some work. This maddened Sullivan, who rushed in and landed twice on the stomach and neck without receiving a return. Corbett's cleverness astonished the sanguine adherents of the 'big bully.'

4. The Champion seemed much worried that his blows failed to find a resting-place, and he looked serious. Corbett's agility was remarkable. He seemed to escape Sullivan's leads with the greatest ease; doing but very little work himself, it became apparent that he was playing a waiting game. Sullivan's leads were wild, and Corbett landed lightly on the neck, the Champion paying no attention to the blow.

5. Sullivan landed on Corbett's chest, and got a counter on the neck. Corbett landed a terrific left-hand punch on the stomach and followed it up with a right-hander in the same spot. Then he attacked the Champion savagely. Blood flew from Sullivan's nose in streams, and he hugged Corbett to save himself; Corbett, however, pushed him away. Both men were bathed in Sullivan's blood, which was flowing freely.

6. Corbett went at his man instantly, but a punch in the ribs caused him to go slow, and some

sparring ensued. Sullivan was weak, and his face was a sight to behold; he had met a man who did not fear him, and knew how to hit. Corbett advanced and landed the left on the stomach. In a clinch, blows were exchanged, but no damage done. Both countered on the jaw, and Sullivan ended it with a right-hand swing that might have terminated the fight had it landed. Corbett's quickness was marvellous; he broke Sullivan's nose with his left, and continued to visit the sore spot, causing John L. to squirm. The punishment was all one-sided.

7. Sullivan's training stood him in hand, for he was strong when time was called, and walked briskly to the centre. Jem then got home a straight left on the big fellow's belly, and advancing cleverly got three in quick succession on the mouth that had uttered so many slurs on the pugilists of the day. Corbett then jabbed his left into the Champion's face, and the audience showed their appreciation by cheering. He landed a right-hander on the jaw. Then he rushed Sullivan to the ropes and fought him to a stand-still.

8. Sullivan made a desperate attempt to force matters, landing his right heavily. Jem did not relish this, because he banged the big fellow on the

jaw, and followed it up with another blow on the nose, getting a good stiff punch over the heart in return. Jem then punched his man twice in the ribs, and got home a terrific right-hand smash on the jaw. Sullivan was weary when time was called, and the expression of his countenance was sufficient proof that defeat was only a question of time.

9. Sullivan's blows were short. Finally he hit Corbett on the ear, the blow sounding throughout the building. The right hand which had brought down so many failed to even jolt Corbett. An exchange of blows followed, Sully putting his right on Corbett's ear once more. Both men clinched, and the Sullivan faction shouted 'foul' in hopes of breaking up the fight. Corbett put his left lightly on the big fellow's cheek, and landed three more blows as the round ended.

10. The men sparred warily. Sullivan put his left on Corbett's ear with force, and ducked a return in good old style. A strong exchange followed, with honours even. Sullivan improving, he caught Corbett on the right eye, reddening the skin, and making Jem knit his brows. Corbett had all the best of an exchange that followed, landing twice on the jaw.

11. Sparring was followed by hot work, Corbett

doing most damage. Protracted sparring ensued. The young man rushed in and had the best of a rally on the ropes. He followed it up with another smash on Sully's nose, retreating each time out of harm's way.

12. Corbett rained blow after blow on Sullivan's stomach, and Sullivan, in attempting to escape, let his guard down and received two blows on the neck and jaw. These were followed by punches in the abdomen. He played for the jaw, but missed twice, and waited for an opening. He landed a terrific right-hander under Sullivan's chin, which, had it been delivered on the point of the jaw, would have ended the fight. Sullivan was now a mere toy in Corbett's hands, and took a fearful beating.

13. Corbett ducked away every time Sullivan attempted to lead. Not a blow was struck till near the end of the round, when Corbett put his left on the big fellow's jaw, springing away out of danger.

14. A sharp exchange began the battle, both landing on the jaw, and then the big fellow smashed Corbett on the cheek with his left. It made no impression on Corbett's hard face, and Jem squared matters with two punches on the mouth and chin. A sharp counter followed, both men landing with fierceness. Corbett jabbed Sullivan on the nose,

and had the best of the rally that followed, his blow having more steam than Sullivan's.

15. Each got home on the neck and jaw, and they mixed it up in lively style, Corbett doing admirable work. The big fellow clinched his teeth in a vicious fashion in hopes of frightening Corbett, but it failed to have the desired effect. It only amused Corbett, who got home on the stomach and got away unhurt. Sullivan's blows were weak. Corbett's full-arm swings had a world of force.

16. John made a dying effort and rushed in, but was met with a straight left-hander on the mouth. Sullivan's breathing was laboured, and could be heard plainly by persons twenty feet from the ring. Corbett punched the big fellow on the mouth, and jabbed his left into the stomach repeatedly, escaping punishment with ease. They clenched, and Corbett hugged his man while the crowd yelled 'foul.' Corbett raised his hands deprecatingly as he broke away. He said, 'Gentlemen, before I get through I'll punish this man so there'll be no question as to who is the Champion.' His speech was well received.

17. There was very little fighting in this round, neither man landing a blow worthy of record. The time was taken up in sparring, and the round was

the tamest of the fight. Sullivan was trying to stave off defeat.

18. Jem jabbed John twice on the short ribs when the big fellow attempted to come in at the opening of the round. Sullivan's nose had stopped bleeding, and his face was much more sightly than half-an-hour before. His mouth was open, for he breathed heavily. John smashed Jem twice on the ear, but the young gladiator responded with two blows on the jaw that were scorchers. Corbett's next blow, a right-hander on the jaw, was a dangerous one, and he followed it with three more of the same kind, and Sullivan's chances waned rapidly. He tried to run away, but was too tired, and had to accept the 'gruel' dealt out to him.

19. Corbett's cleverness in tapping Sullivan and getting away was greatly admired up to this time, and when he jabbed the big fellow four times on the face in succession the spectators raised a howl. Sullivan got in his left on Corbett's breast, but it was merely a tap. Then Corbett touched John L. up for two right-handers on the body, amid more howls. The people seemed to be with Corbett. They realized the big Boston Blower was in for a sound thrashing, and enjoyed seeing the medicine dealt out to him.

20. Corbett fought his man to the ropes, using his left and right on stomach and jaw. He punished the big man repeatedly in his wind, and it seemed to be all day with Sullivan, who carried his right hand as though it had been injured: it wasn't though. His arms were tired, and the gloves pulled them down. Jem jabbed the big fellow in the stomach again, and then came in, getting home on the ear and ribs with great force. Corbett had a marked advantage when time was called, amid deafening cheers.

21. Corbett was out for blood, and started to finish the man who had held the championship for so many years, and whose name was a terror to all. He rushed in and planted blow after blow on Sullivan's face and neck. The Champion, so soon to lose his coveted title, backed away, trying to save himself. He lowered his guard from sheer exhaustion, and catching a fearful smash on the jaw reached to the ropes, and the blood poured down his face in torrents, and made a crimson river across the broad chest. His eyes were glassy, and it was a mournful act when the young Californian shot his right across the jaw and Sullivan fell like an ox.

It was a game battle, but Sullivan was clearly

out-fought; in fact he was never in the hunt. It was a triumph of science and agility over strength and physical power. Corbett forced the fighting from start to finish. He landed on Sullivan when and where he pleased.

Sullivan's nose was broken, his face and body bruised, and he was finally battered down, a bleeding mass of humanity, unable to rise at the call of time. Sullivan stood up against the greatest number of hard blows ever received in the ring, and showed himself to be the game man his friends knew him. Corbett was wholly uninjured, and was as fresh as ever at the finish. Sullivan had failed to land even one of his famous swinging right-hand blows."

In this fight the Californian had the advantage of youth, and was probably in far better condition than Sullivan, so that, having escaped serious damage in the first few rounds, he had a tired and stale opponent to deal with, and had no difficulty in finishing him off as he pleased. The result went far to demonstrate that a big man in indifferent training, who promises to "knock out" any one in such and such a number of rounds, will be unfit for anything after the specified number of rounds spent in "hurricane" fighting.

CHAPTER VIII.

TIMING AND COUNTERING.

THE amount of actual and effective work done in any fight by judicious "timing" or countering is hard to detect. There is far more in it than meets the eye, for it is often next to impossible to say which man really gets the worst of such and such a counter. You may see both heads fly back from the force of the simultaneous hit, or one may be apparently moved the greater space and yet not receive the worst jerk. Of course the man who leads or attacks should receive the most credit, though it often happens that he gets the worst of it from the force he has put into his own hit.

The following extract from my handbook in Messrs. Bell and Co.'s "All England Series" seems to fairly emphasize the importance of the subject, and the following portion of Chapter VII. in that volume is therefore quoted in full—

"There is nothing in the art which requires greater accuracy of eye, and knowledge of reach and speed, than this very delicate operation of timing. You somehow find out, partly by intuition and partly through the experience of a round or two, what sort of speed your opponent possesses, and you also take his measure as to reach. If you ascertain that you are slightly quicker and possess a longer reach, then watch carefully for the slightest movement on his part, and the very instant you perceive such movement, hit out bang at his head with your left. You will reach him first, and the blow will be the more severe to him as he meets it in his effort to reach you. In this case make no attempt at guarding, it is unnecessary; keep your right well in reserve for his ribs or for a cross-counter, should he try a second hit before retreating. You can seldom properly 'time' a man with the cross-counter *to start with*, it is generally after he has led off with his left, and his left is well past your head, that your right comes in on his left ear or the point of the jaw, and, for preference, let it be the latter.

".The above applies when you possess the advantage both in speed and length of reach. Next suppose that you are only better in rapidity;

then, *cæteris paribus*, you should still pursue the same tactics, for always remember that the smallest fraction of a second determines who shall be the recipient of the 'kick' in a hit. At the same time, in this case, you will do well to throw up your guard as you hit, or, in my opinion, better still, dodge your head smartly to the right at the moment of delivering the blow. You will thus, in the latter case, still have your right arm over your mark in case the enemy should have feinted at your head, and, should he really have gone at your head, you will be better prepared, when his left has passed harmlessly over your left shoulder, to put in a good hit on his jaw, or else to visit his left short ribs with a well-tucked in punch.

"Don't try 'timing' if you are both about equal in speed, but you may occasionally do so if you are a little better in the matter of reach. I say don't try timing where there is not much to choose between yourself and your opponent, because, if you do so, a slogging match of no great interest is likely to be the result.

"What are you to do when your opponent is superior in speed, but about equal to you in reach? It is a much harder matter to answer this question; for relative weight, strength, and condition must have a great deal to say in respect to the tactics to be employed; though, as a general rule, I have no hesitation in saying that you should act on the defensive, for, when you hit, the other man hits, and, as previously shown, reaches you first. Better try to make the best use of your guard, and look out for a favourable opportunity for popping in two or three good ones, and then get away.

"If two men are equally matched as regards size, weight, and experience, and one possesses the superiority in speed whilst the other has a better reach, I should certainly back the quicker man: supposing, of course, that both have mastered the rudiments, and can hit equally straight.

"Depend upon it a *very* quick man, and therefore a good timer, even if he only weighs eleven stone, is a nasty customer to tackle. You don't know what to do with him, for the very instant you are on the point of pulling off something grand, out pops his left, bang on your nose, with all the weight of his body to back it up. His head is never where you want it to be, and if by chance you get well home on his body it is probably at the expense of a rapid return on your short ribs or side of the head. The delicacy of judgment which can be brought into play in the very practical work of timing can only be appreciated by an old hand, and whilst on this portion of the subject, let me warn beginners not to be discouraged at finding themselves constantly stopping a good timer's left with their faces. They should go on trying to improve their speed and straight hitting, never for a moment losing sight of the definition of a straight line; but let them avoid boxing with *very* inferior performers, or with those extremely objectionable superior ones who try to 'show-off,' and really damage them and discourage them from learning.

"Always try to get the best man you know to take you on now and again; if he is strong in the art, he will probably be merciful, and will, if he is a good fellow, try to give you the best advice in preference to rattling your ivories and making you see stars and stripes. But, having thus secured the assistance of a good professional or clever amateur, when you are taking the lesson from him never be tempted to rush at him in a shabby attempt to knock him out. Should you do so, he will probably retreat two or three times in order to save you, and then, when you repeat the experiment, he will, as likely as not, time you, and put a stop to such liberties. Remember that you are taking a lesson, and be considerate to one who is trying to help you along, and who may experience much difficulty in preventing you from punishing yourself."

Some important fights have been very remarkable for steady punching without much attempt at guarding or avoiding, and it has then generally resulted in a victory for the best punishment-taker. It will also be noticed that in such cases the men have been fairly well matched both as to weight and height, for no sane and well-advised man would dream of trusting to mere exchanges, blow for blow, with a taller and heavier adversary.

Take it, then, as axiomatic, that, when it comes to countering, and you find your opponent can reach you a fractional part of a second before you reach him, that you should at once alter your game, probably trying for close half-arm work or for feints. When, in the great fights of the past, victory has smiled on a man not by any means the favourite, the result has as often as not been brought about by a clear-headed conception of such questions as these, for the victor has outgeneralled his opponent by adopting the correct tactics at the right time.

A distinction must be drawn between "timing" and "countering," though they are so nearly allied as to be almost inseparable. Timing is, strictly speaking, when you judge you can reach your man first and hit out, with that intent, just as he is hitting out. You beat him in "time," or hope so to do.

Fig. 6. The Counter.

The counter generally takes effect when a man has either missed his mark, as in the case of the cross-counter, or when both men are recipients of a portion of the hit, *e.g.* both leading with the left or right at the same time, and both landing with more or less effect.

CROSS COUNTER I.

CHAPTER IX.

THE CROSS-COUNTER AND KNOCK-OUT BLOWS.

IN the ordinary counter proper both men hit with the same hand, *i.e.* both with the left, as in the illustration on p. 198, or both with the right. In the cross-counter the right or left arm *crosses* the left or right of the opponent in the lead off: *vide* illustrations. In the cross-counter, which usually occurs in practice, the left lead—and this especially when the man leading hits very straight—passes over your *right* shoulder, you duck slightly to the left and bring in your right over his left shoulder, catching him somewhere on the left-hand side of his jaw or head.

This hit cannot properly be called a straight hit, because the arm is half turned round so as to bring the hitting knuckles uppermost, and the line followed by the fist is strictly a curve known as a "spiral"; but the arm *at the moment of the hit getting home* is straight and stiff. It is not a hook hit, nor will it be a half-arm hit unless your man has over-reached himself, and got to very close quarters indeed. It is the spiral form of the curve which enables you just to "get in," avoiding his left shoulder, and, as it were, getting over both his arm and shoulder. You should not shift the right foot, and one reason why this foot should be well to the right of the line on which your left is planted is, that it gives you great additional power for this cross-counter. As soon as ever the spiral hit has landed, and indeed *at the instant of its so landing*, the weight of your body with full force of spring from the right foot should be felt in the blow.

A short consideration of the position, mechanically, will be instructive.

Your opponent has missed you in his lead and his forward step, as indicated in Fig. 7, has left him in a particularly unstable condition to receive hits in the direction indicated by the arrow. In other words, it will be understood that the base A B C has been lengthened by his reach out to A', and his head, with nearly *the whole weight of his body, is vertically over the narrowest and most unstable portion of the triangular base.* Your position, on the other hand, is as stable as ever, and you suddenly bringing a great *portion* of your weight, backed by a powerful spring from the right foot, to bear on the opponent's weakest point, *i.e.* that point where the application of force can most easily upset him. What wonder, then, that so many men are floored by the cross-counter?

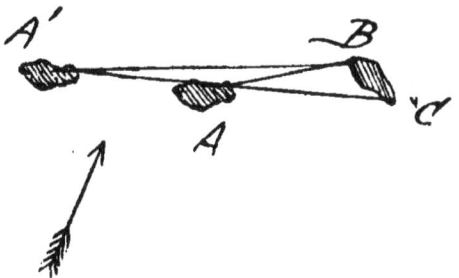

Fig. 7. Cross-Counter and Knock-out Blows.

It is not, as many suppose, that the cross-counter is such a hard hit, for it is not nearly, *cæteris paribus*, as hard as the lead off with the *whole* weight of the body behind it; it is simply that it catches the adversary where he is mechanically weakest, and so topples him over. Of course when the hit happens to land well on the "point of the jaw," it is worse in its effects than when it lands higher up.

Some of those who gave me the advantage of

their opinions on my former little work, took exception to the description of the cross-counter therein contained. One of the illustrations gives the left-hand lead passing over the *left* shoulder of the man using the cross-counter. This, it was held, is incorrect; but I feel I must maintain the position, since the arms really do cross, the only difference being that the leader has, as most men do, hit slightly across and so pulled his hit towards his opponent's left shoulder. Note here the danger of the duck to the left when you are going to use the cross-counter; most men hitting across you are so apt to duck on to the lead, and if you do so, good-bye to your chance of pulling off a good "cross." It is only wise to duck to the left when your man is a very straight hitter indeed, and even then you have to more or less chance his upper cut with the right.

The cross-counter is answerable for the sending to sleep of many a good man, for it is a side hit, and, as such, is more dangerous than any flush hit excepting only that on the *mark*, of which more anon.

If you find a man constantly cross-countering you, it is a good plan to draw him on by a feint with your left, and then, just as he is coming in

CROSS COUNTER II.

with his right, duck well to the left and come in on his face with *your* right. Then what was originally intended for a cross-counter to his credit becomes a true counter to yours.

It always seems to me that the cross-counter often proves a sort of compensation or make-up to a man who is fighting an up-hill battle against very straight left-hand hitting. If the left-hand lead is remarkably straight and rarely pulled across, the slight duck to the left may often be resorted to, and the right-hand cross-counter be brought in with great effect.

You should not frequently use the cross-counter, but hold it in reserve as a surprise: it may come in very handy too when you are getting tired of a long spell of left-hand work. When rather exhausted it is an actual relief to change the *form* of your exertion—ample examples of this are seen in swimming and other branches of athletics.

Probably the cross-counter is seen at its greatest advantage when opposed to a "choppy" left-hand lead. The tendency of the chop being to bring the left shoulder low and jerk the head forward on to the right-hand cross. But, fortunately for the art, and to the credit of modern exponents, the chopping style is hardly ever met with amongst boxers of any repute in the present day.

The habit of systematically playing for knock-out blows is probably rather against the encouragement of first-class style. It may be all very well for a certain fighter of great strength and gluttony to match himself to knock out all and any comers in so many rounds in such and such a ring. Here is a definite challenge; it is like killing rats in a saw-pit: "I back my dog to kill forty rats in twenty minutes, and lay them all out in a row;" and to a certain limited extent it is interesting. When, however, it comes to looking for the knock-out blow, and for that alone, in each and every contest, amateur and professional alike, it seems possible that all-round fighting may, in time, suffer deterioration.

We all know that the knock-out hit has overtaken the better man over and over again, but take the annals of fights right away through, and you will find judgmatic fighters like Tom Sayers, Nat Langham, and Jem Mace considered every point, and, whilst quite ready to knock out any adversary at the first opportunity, were loth to give themselves away or unduly expose themselves in the attempt to administer what, after all, *might* not prove an effective knock-out.

A good deal depends on the state of exhaustion of the "knockee": in some cases, where both men have fought to a stand-still, it has been a mere matter of chance who shall administer the slight tap or even push which shall practically send the other to sleep.

More, as a rule, depends upon the portion of the anatomy visited; the "point of the jaw" and the "mark" being the two tender spots. Corbett sent the great J. L. to the land of oblivion by a cross on the jaw, and he himself was rendered *hors de combat* by Fitzsimmons' severe body-blows—especially by that which landed on the mark.

Then there is another aspect of the question. The idea of men never meeting in a competition, without the expectation of either being rendered insensible or the hope of rendering some other friendly competitor insensible, is not altogether a pleasant idea, and it is suggested that it may in time interfere with those pleasant and quite friendly competitions where men spar for points and an exhibition of good form.

In the professional contest each man does his best to thoroughly disable his antagonist, but in the amateur trial of skill this should not be so. As hinted above, I doubt if the great hunt for knock-out blows is advisable even for prize-fighters—and I cannot think that it will bring the amateurs any advantages—it is almost sure to give a handle to the sensitive and superior persons alluded to in my opening remarks, and thus may tend to injure the art by bringing it again into disfavour.

CROSS COUNTER WITH LEFT.

CHAPTER X.

RIGHT-HANDED BOXERS.

FROM time to time men have appeared in the ring and elsewhere, who prefer to stand with the right leg and arm advanced instead of the left. Such men are more hard to tackle, for the very obvious reason that they have had plenty of practice with those standing in the ordinary way, whilst the every-day boxer seldom meets the right-handed customer.

Always look upon the advent of these rare birds with satisfaction, and take every opportunity of sparring with them, for the experience to be gained in this way is very much to be desired. Your best plan is to work round to the left instead of to the right, for by this means you stand a chance of avoiding right-hand leads.

One of the most obvious and effective attacks is a duck to the left with a good step in and right-handed hit at the mark, following it up, *à la* Tom Sayers, with a flush hit in the face with the same hand. His best reply to this attack is either to cover his mark with his left and counter you with his right, or to just avoid the blow and come in with right and left on your head.

You may often very effectually cross-counter a man standing right foot first; he leads as usual with his right at your head, the blow passes over your left shoulder, and you bring in your left over his right shoulder and on the point of the jaw or side of head in the usual manner. In getting away there may be a risk of an upper cut from his left, so you should keep your right ready for a stop.

Probably the best-known right-handed fighter— one of the top sawyers of the Ring in the second quarter of the present century—was William Thompson, or "Bendigo" as he was known to his pals. In taking up his position he was wont to stand rather square towards his opponent, but with the right arm the most advanced. By adopting this position he was probably more ready for right and left hitting, but he was more liable to be knocked over backwards, as, indeed, he very frequently was.

Do not on any account try to equalize matters by

DUCK TO THE RIGHT, WITH LEFT-HAND HIT AT MARK.

standing with *your* right foot and hand first, for you will do the very opposite. Stand in your usual way and make the best of a bad job; if your right-handed man is a good 'un he will make it unpleasant for you, unless, which is extremely unlikely, you have had a great deal of practice with such men. Always take them on for *practice*, when you can get them; but never in a *fight* where it can be avoided!

CHAPTER XI.

FEINTS.

NO greater mistake can be made by a teacher than that of allowing his pupils to box "free" too often. When beginners are allowed to go in for feinting, the study of which should be reserved for advanced pupils who have acquired a good style through long practice, they soon develop a shockingly bad and undecided style.

This is obvious, that the more you can put your adversary off his guard the better, and the object of the feint is to make him think you are about to do one thing when you really intend to do something quite different. But, whatever you are to do, you should first know *how to do it*, so that if you let a man feint before he knows how to hit, it is obviously putting the cart before the horse.

Instruct well and carefully in the fundamental principles, and first see that your man can really put his advancing, retreating, and straight-hitting into practice, and then, when satisfied that he can judge distances and put your teaching to *practical* proof, let him tackle the intricate question of feinting.

It is necessary here to repeat and emphasize the importance of never taking your eyes from those of your adversary, though it has been suggested, that if you *look* at a certain part it will convey the impression that you are going to hit at that part. No one of any experience would be taken in by this dodge. Keep the eyes where they are, and the slightest movement of the hand should be sufficient to indicate the feint. Say you have been leading off with the left at the head several times consecutively; your opponent will expect the next blow to be the same, but it will in reality be your feint, and you will duck to the right, and bring in your left on the mark. This is feint at head with body-blow.

Or you may feint at the body and come in under the jaw. This is a good feint, and, if the hit gets home, it is often a " punisher," as you hit *up* with a great spring from the right foot;

and may lift the adversary altogether off his feet, so that in falling he may either sit down, or the back of his head may be the first part which reaches the ground: it is a satisfactory hit, but it must be noted that if the other man is handy with his right, a cross-counter may make you sorry you did not try some other game.

The above are examples of single feints. It is often well to try a feint, say with the right, and then come in with the left. A good feint would be at the head with the left, and duck to left and come in on the left side, just above the belt, with the right only; in this case you are rather open to a visitation in the shape of an upper cut from the adversary's right.

Mr. Robert Fitzsimmons, who has fairly won his way up to the highest distinction as a fair and unusually scientific fighter, is reported to have given the following account of some of the feints he has from time to time made use of—

"The blow that put Sharkey out after repeatedly fouling me in the most unfair fight that was ever seen in the prize-ring, was a left and right, which had him dazed. I feinted with my left and he threw up both arms around his face to protect himself, which left a clean opening for a left-hand shift on the stomach. This blow did the job. It knocked the wind out of him, which brought him forward. I quickly shot the same hand up under his chin and knocked him out. I leave it to the public whether this was a fair blow or not. The first time I defeated Peter Maher I feinted with my left. He tried to cross me with the right. I pulled my head back, and then delivered a left-hand punch in the mouth. His right was spent across his chest, which left me a clean opening, and he had no guard. I kept this kind of punching up for eleven rounds, at the end of which he quit. The second time we met, after deliberately fouling me three times, Maher had his left arm around my neck, and was punching me in the stomach. I was crouched down and up close to him, ready to deliver my right when the opportunity presented itself. Maher let go of my neck and swung his left downward to his side, thus giving him more power to land his left on my jaw, and giving me the opening I was waiting for. I parried his right swing and jolted him on the jaw with my right, a distance of about six inches, which knocked him down and out, and won me the title of Champion of the World. In the fight with Jem Hall I delivered a blow over his kidney with the right hand which made him wince. I was about to repeat the same thing, when he threw his elbow down to stop the blow, and swung his right at me at the same time. I quickly saw an opening for his jaw, and instead of landing on his elbow I changed the direction of my blow, and landed on his jaw, knocking him out. I had Dempsey in a corner, all but knocked out. I feinted with my left. He tried to stop me, but was too weak, and I let him go past me, and then I put my right under his ear, standing behind him at the same time I delivered the blow."

It is highly probable that Fitzsimmons, who evidently lays out his plan of campaign with great care and skill, manages to keep his head clear *during the progress of a fight*, and this is what so few men can do. Tom Sayers was very sound in this direction; being himself a middle weight, and being constantly in danger of being "cornered" by the heavy men he tackled and defeated one after another, his wits were brightened, and all the resources at his command were brought forward to a remarkable degree.

Not having actually *seen* the fights, one is rather at a disadvantage, but it seems highly probable that Tom's "double," so frequently alluded to as his favourite hit, was often in reality a "feint" at the body followed up by a hit in the face or under the jaw. This is a very good way of opening the ball at a competition if you have reason to believe that your opponent is quite unprepared for this line of attack, and expects you to do a great deal of sparring round for an opening. You may thus get in the first blow—always an advantage, since it annoys the other man, and makes you feel quite pleased with yourself.

CHAPTER XII.

FOUL PLAY.

FROM "roughing on the ropes" to "eye-gouging," the history of the Ring abounds in instances and examples of foul play, and from the days of Fig, nearly two hundred years ago, to the present time it has been the aim and object of all lovers of the art to define and punish this kind of thing, and amend the rules so as to minimize the chances of any degeneration of pugilism in the direction of cruelty or brutality.

In looking through accounts of some of the earlier fights one's ideas of fair play, as now understood, receive many shocks. Even that superior person, Mr. John Jackson, who flourished between 1788 and 1795, was capable of a little scragging on occasions, for, when he met the redoubtable Dan Mendoza in 1795, and fought him for two hundred guineas aside, we read that in the fifth round

"Jackson caught his opponent by the hair, and holding him down, gave him several severe blows, which brought him to the ground; Mendoza's friends called 'foul,' but the umpires decided on the contrary. Odds had now changed 2 to 1 on Jackson." This account, like many others, is a little ambiguous, as it does not, at first sight, appear possible to hold a man down by the hair, then give him several smashes, and ultimately bring him to the ground. Possibly it means that poor Mendoza, being already held on the ground by the hair, was metaphorically brought even lower still, by being there knocked into a state of insensibility. The more probable interpretation is that Jackson got him on the ropes, held him there by superior force, and punched him till he fell in a senseless heap. In any case it is strange that a man of Jackson's science and general aptitude for teaching the noble art should have resorted to such tactics.

Then there is the account of a fight which took place between two well-known men in very wet weather, when the mud in the ring was more plentiful than pleasant, and there were several slips and falls. One of the partisans whispered to his friend who was struggling on the ground with his opponent: "Why don't yer close his peepers with a handful of mud?" On another much more recent occasion two pugilistic friends were contending on the ground, when one was heard to exclaim with fervour, "Don't gouge my eye out, Charlie!"

In the very early days of the Ring, one John Slack, after defeating Jack Broughton, was matched against a gigantic Frenchman, named Pettit, and the following rather amusing account of the contest appeared in 1751—

"At the first set-to Pettit seized Slack by the throat, held him up against the rails, and *grained* him so much as to make him extremely black. This continued for half a minute, before Slack could break from Pettit's hold; after which, for near ten minutes, Pettit kept fighting and driving hard at Slack, when at length Slack closed with his antagonist, and gave him a severe fall, after that a second and a third, but between these falls, Pettit threw Slack twice off the stage; indeed Pettit so much dreaded Slack's falls, that he ran directly at his hams and tumbled him down, and by that means gave Slack an opportunity of making the falls easy. When they had been fighting eighteen minutes the odds ran against

Slack, a guinea to a shilling; whereas, on first setting out, it was three or four to one on his head; but after this time Slack *shortened* Pettit, so as to disable him from running and throwing him down in the manner he had done before, but obliged him to stand to *close fighting*. Slack then closed one of his eyes, and beat him very much about the face; at twenty minutes Pettit grew weaker and Slack stronger. This was occasioned by Slack's straight way of fighting. At twenty-two minutes the best judges allowed Slack to have the advantage over Pettit very considerably, as he was then *recovering his wind*, owing to his game qualities. When they had boxed twenty-four minutes, Pettit once more threw Slack over the rails. This, indeed, Slack allowed him to do, for as he got his hold, Slack fired a blow under Pettit's ribs that hurt severely. While Slack was again getting upon the stage (it was not half a minute before he remounted), Pettit had so much the fear of his antagonist before his eyes, that he walked off without so much as civilly taking leave of the spectators. The cockers called this rogueing it, for it is generally thought that Pettit ran away full strong. The whole time of their fighting was twenty-five minutes, and this morning the battle was judged to Slack, who drew the first ten guineas out of the box."

This is a fairly jumbled and confused account of what must have been a *bonâ fide* rough-and-tumble match in which stamina and hitting powers came off victorious.

In quite recognized fights for the Championship we are constantly reading of falls in order to escape punishment, and of those other falls in which the knee, elbow, or shoulder played so prominent a part. It was quite part of the tactics of some of the old fighters to fall upon the prostrate foe in such a manner that the angular points above-named were brought into severe contact with the most vital portions of the antagonist's anatomy. Thus, coming down kneeling hard on a man's chest or falling with the elbow or shoulder on his mark or abdomen, often prejudiced his chances of rising within the specified time.

On occasions the ropes have been cut or lowered by the partisans of men who were being unduly bashed, squeezed, or in danger of being throttled. When Sayers was being hugged on the ropes by Heenan, the ropes were lowered, and, according to the then existing rules of the Ring, this was not altogether out of order. Rule 28 of the Ring Code prescribed that—

"Where a man shall have his antagonist across the ropes in such a position as to be helpless, and to endanger his life by strangulation or apoplexy, it shall be in the power of the referee to direct the seconds to take their man away, and thus conclude the round; and that the man or his seconds refusing to obey the direction of the referee shall be deemed the loser."

The fact is that ropes were primarily intended to keep the men within a certain prescribed limit, to prevent one or other running away unduly, and to keep the space clear of too eager spectators. All this points to the prevention of any *lateral* or horizontal pressure; the moment there is any *vertical* pressure, as in the case of men using the ropes as supports, or getting an adversary down and squeezing him by super-imposed pressure and weight, then we say that the functions of the ropes are being abused, and that they should be at once lowered or cut.

In considering this question of what constitutes foul play it is hardly necessary to say that all kicking is forbidden, as are all hits below the belt. In the French style, *la Savate*, you may hit or kick a man everywhere from the crown of his head to the soles of his feet, so that there is a delightful freedom and immunity from the restraints which hamper *le boxe* as practised in perfidious Albion.

In the annals of the Ring there are numerous examples of men going down to avoid punishment, and yet the fatal word "foul" has not been pronounced by the referee; but the following account, which will form a fitting termination to this chapter, shows that this was not always the case, for the referee, Mr. Osbaldiston, familiarly known as the "Old Squire," gave his decision without much hesitation against the man who repeatedly and wilfully abused the rules of the Ring.

This fight took place in April 1845, between two "big 'uns," Caunt and Bendigo, the former being 33 years of age and scaling just under 14st., and the latter being 36 years old and weighing just over 12st. Both men had trained carefully and were supposed to be in the very pink of condition.

CAUNT *v.* BENDIGO.

"*Round* 1. Caunt threw himself into attitude erect and smiling, whilst Bendigo at once began to play round him, dodging and shifting ground in his usual style. Caunt let fly his left, but missed. Bendigo, active on his pins, retreated, and *chasséed* left and right; at last he crept in closer, then out again, till, watching his opportunity, he got closer, and popped in a sounding smack with his left on Caunt's right eye. After a few lively capers he succeeded in delivering another crack with his left on Caunt's cheek, opening the old scar left by Brassey, and drawing first blood, as well as producing an electric effect on Caunt's optic. (Shouts unlimited from Bendigo's friends.) Bendy got away laughing, and again played round his man. Caunt got closer, missed an intended slasher with his left, and closed for the fall. Bendy grappled with him, but could not escape, and Caunt, by superior strength, forced him down at the corner.

2. Caunt up at the call of time, his cheek and eye testifying the effects of the visitations in the last round, Bendy dancing round him, and waiting for an opening. Slight exchanges left and right, Caunt missing his opponent's head; Bendigo, in retreating to the ropes, slipped down, was up again in a moment, and dashed to his man. Wild exchanges, but no apparent execution; Caunt hit out viciously left and right, missed his kind intentions, and Bendy got down unscathed.

3. Caunt came up quiet, and determined on annihilation. Bendy again played about him, but did not get near enough for execution. After some wild passes, Caunt missing, Bendigo, on the retreat, was caught in the powerful grasp of Caunt, who threw him across the ropes, and fell on him, but no mischief done. (Shouts from the roughs.)

4. Caunt came up blowing, when Bendigo, after a little dodging, popped in his left under his guard, and got away. Caunt, determined on mischief, followed his man, and at last getting to him let fly left and right, catching Bendy with the left on the mouth slightly, but missing his right. Bendigo finding himself in difficulties got down, falling on the ropes, and grinning facetiously at Goliath the second, who walked back to his corner.

5. Caunt, first to lead off, drew on his man, but Bendy retreated, Caunt after him, till he reached the ropes, when Caunt hit out left and right, his blows passing harmlessly over Bendigo's head. There was a want of precision in Caunt's hitting not to be accounted for, with his supposed science. Bendigo, who stopped rather wildly, got down.

6. Caunt, first to the call of time, waited with his hands well up, but blowing. We believe he was over-trained, and really distressed thus early

in the struggle. Bendy manœuvred to the right and left; Caunt approached him, but he retreated. Caunt let fly left and right, but Bendy ducked his canister, and got down with more caution than gallantry.

7. Left-handed exchanges on the nobs, but of no moment. Caunt made some desperate lunges left and right, but was too high, and Bendy slipped down.

8. Bendy after a few dodges got within Caunt's guard with his left, and gave him a pretty prop on the cheek. Caunt missed his return, but, seizing Bendy in his grasp, flung him over the ropes. Here he leaned heavily on him, overbalanced himself, and fell over on his own head, bringing Bendy with him, amidst loud shouts and abusive epithets. Caunt fell at the feet of his friends, Tom Spring and the Editor of *Bell's Life*, the latter of whom was seated on that side of the ring near the centre stake.

9. Bendy came up full of glee, and played round his man, watching for his opportunity to plant his left. This at last offered, and catching Caunt on the old wound he ducked his head to avoid the return, and got down.

10. More sly manœuvring by Bendy, who, after

dancing about at arm's-length, stole a march, and caught Caunt a stinging smack with his left on the right cheek, drawing more claret, and giving the big 'un more of the tragedy hue. Caunt instantly closed, gave Bendy the Cornish hug, flung him by main strength, and fell on him.

11. Bendy pursued his eccentric gyrations round his man, when with the swiftness of lightning he popped in his left on the jaw and right on the body, and fell. Caunt, stung by these visitations, followed him, and dropped on his knees close to his man, but luckily did not touch him, and Bendy was picked up laughing and uninjured; in fact, up to this time he scarce showed the semblance of a hit, beyond a slight contusion on the lip and left ear.

12. Bendigo retreated from Caunt's vigorous charge right and left, and slipped down, but instantly jumped up and resumed the round. After some wild fighting, but no execution worth recording, Bendy went down in his corner, amidst cries of 'Foul!' 'Unmanly,' etc.

13. Caunt, on coming to the scratch, let fly with his left, just grazing the top of Bendigo's scalp. A sharp rally followed, and counter-hits with the left were exchanged, Bendy hitting Caunt with such

terrible force on the old spot on the right cheek that he knocked him clean off his legs, thus gaining the first knock-down blow, amidst deafening shouts from the Nottingham roughs. Bendigo's blow was so powerful that he actually rebounded back against the stakes, and Caunt was picked up almost stunned by the severity of the visitation.

14. Bendy, elated with his handiwork in the last round, again dashed in with his left, but not being sufficiently quick in his retreat, Caunt caught him round the neck with his left and lifted him to the ropes, and there hung on him till, in trying to escape from his grasp, he pulled him forward, threw, and fell heavily on him, amidst the indignant shouts of his opponents.

15. Bendy came up as lively as a kitten, while Caunt, undismayed, came smiling to the scratch. Caunt plunged in his left and right, but missed; he then seized his man for the throw, but Bendy slipped round, and seizing Caunt by the neck pulled him down.

16. Bendy tried his left-hand dodge, but missed and retreated. Caunt followed him up to his corner, hitting out right and left, but throwing his hands too high. Caunt grappled for the fall, but Bendy got down, Caunt following suit, and as he

sat upon the ground, beckoned Bendy to come to him.

17. Bendy made himself up for mischief, and played round his man for a few seconds, when, getting within distance, he delivered a terrific hit with his left on Caunt's mouth, and fell. Caunt's upper lip was completely split by this blow, and the blood flowed in torrents from the wound. (Renewed cheers from the Nottingham division.)

18. Bendy again came the artful dodge, put in his left on Caunt's mouth, and fell. Caunt pointed at him, but Bendy laughed and nodded.

19. Bendy, more cautious, kept out; Caunt rushed to him, hitting out left and right, but with little effect. Bendy retreated. Caunt caught him on the ropes, and hung on him till he fell. (More shouting and some threats at Caunt.)

20. Caunt, anxious to be at work, advanced, while Bendy retreated to the ropes, where he hit up with his left, and slipped. Caunt turned his back, and was retiring, when Bendy jumped up, and had another slap at him. Caunt turned round and caught him under his arm as he attempted to escape, lifted him to the ropes, and there held him till he fell, amidst the cries of Bendy's friends.

21. Caunt, prompt to the call of time, his hands

well up, but Bendy again stole a march, popped in his left, and slipped down to avoid a return of the compliment. (Indignant expressions at Bendigo's shifty way of terminating the rounds.)

22. Bendy was still free from punishment, and looked as fresh as when he entered the ring, while Caunt, although firm and active on his pins, showed heavy marks of punishment on his frontispiece; his cheek had a gaping wound, his lip cut, and eye and nose evincing the consequence of Bendy's sly but stinging visitations. Caunt, impatient at Bendy's out-fighting, rushed to him left and right, but Bendy, unwilling to try the weight of superior metal, slipped down, and Caunt fell over him, but not on him, as his friends anticipated, and as perhaps he intended.

23. Both fresh. After a little dodging, advancing and retreating, Bendy again nailed Caunt with his left on his damaged kissing-trap. Caunt caught him a slight nobber on the head with his left, and Bendy got down.

24. Bendy again played round his man till within distance, when he popped in a heavy blow on the ribs with his left and got down without a return. There was an immediate cry of 'Foul!' and an appeal was made to the referee. He

hesitated, amidst tumultuous cries of 'Fair! fair!' and allusions to the size of Caunt. The uproar was terrific, and the inner circle was overwhelmed by the roughs from without rushing in to enforce their arguments in favour of Bendy. At last the referee decided 'Fair!' and time was called.

25. Nick Ward was here so overcome with his exertions that he was taken out of the ring and his office was filled by Nobby Clark. The moment time was called, and Bendy reached the scratch, Caunt rushed to him left and right, and after slight and wild exchanges with the left, Bendy slipped and got down cunning.

26. Bendy, after a little hanky-panky manœuvring, popped in his left on Caunt's mug, and retreated to the corner of the ring. Caunt followed him with so much impetuosity that he hit his hand against the stake. In the close and scramble for the fall, Bendy succeeded in pulling Caunt down, falling with him.

27. Caunt on his guard, his hands well up. Bendy stepped in, delivered his left on the old spot, and dropped to avoid; Caunt shaking his finger at him as he retired to his corner. Caunt's right was visibly puffed by its contact with the stake in the previous round.

28. Caunt attempted to lead off with his left, but Bendy retreated to the ropes, over which Caunt forced him, and as he lay upon him, both still hanging on the lower rope, Bendy hit up with his left. In this position they lay, half in and half out of the ring, till released by their seconds.

29. Caunt let fly left and right, but he was short, Bendy playing the shifty game. Wild fighting on both sides, till Caunt fell on his knees. Bendy looked at him, lifted his hand to strike, but he prudently withheld the blow, and walked to his corner. (Shouts from the Nottingham 'Lambs.')

30. A rally, in which both fought wildly, Caunt catching Bendy a crack over the right brow, from which the claret flowed, and Bendy returning the compliment on Caunt's smeller. In the end Bendy slipped down, and, on rising, a small black patch was placed on the damaged thatch of his peeper.

31. Bendy resumed his hitting and getting down system, popping in his left on Caunt's muzzle, and slipping down.

32. The same game repeated. Spring, indignant, appealed to the referee; and Molineaux, in like manner, called on the umpires for their decision; they disagreed, and Molineaux ran to the referee. The roughs again had their say. A blow

was aimed at Spring's head with a bludgeon, which fortunately only fell on his shoulder. It was a spiteful rap, and he felt the effect of it for some days. The referee declared, however, that he had not seen anything unfair, and Molineaux returned to his man, and brought him to the scratch at the call of time, amidst tremendous confusion, sticks in operation in all directions, and many expressing great dissatisfaction at Bendy's unfair mode of fighting, and the reluctance of the referee to decide against him.

33. A short round, in which Bendy retreated, and Caunt, following, caught him at the ropes, and threw him over, falling on him.

34. Bendy again popped in his left, and threw himself down. This was repeated in the two succeeding rounds, but Bendy's friends attributed it to accident, and not design, and there was no adverse decision on the part of the referee, whose position, amidst the tumult that prevailed, was far from enviable. He must have been possessed of no small nerve to have presumed to decide against the arguments that were so significantly shaken in the vicinity of his knowledge-box, and to this must be attributed his reluctance to give a candid opinion. [Partisan writing.—Ed. *Pugilistica.*]

37. Bendy tried his hit and get down practice, but Caunt seized him round the neck, threw, and fell over him.

38. A wild and scrambling rally, in which Bendigo caught it on the nob. After a scramble they fell, Caunt within and Bendigo without the ropes, when each put his tongue out at the other like angry boys.

39. A slight exchange of hits with the left, when Bendy went down laughing.

40. Bendy popped in his left on Caunt's ancient wound, his right on the ribs, and slipped down.

41. Bendy renewed his left-handed visitation, and was retreating, when Caunt rushed after him, caught him at the ropes, over which he threw him, and fell on him. A blow was here aimed at Caunt's head by one of the roughs with a bludgeon, but it fell on Bendy's shoulder.

42. Exchanges of hits left and right, when Bendy got down.

43. Bendy manœuvred in his old way, delivered a smashing hit with his left on Caunt's throat, and went down to avoid a return.

44. Caunt came up fresh, and rushed to the assault, but Bendy got down. Caunt, indignant, jumped over him, but luckily fell on his knees

beyond him, without touching him. It was assumed that he meant to jump on him, and an uproarious appeal of 'Foul!' was made to the referee, which, after much confusion, he decided in the negative, and ordered the men to go on.

45. Bendy renewed his Merry Andrew curvetings, and tried his left, but Caunt seized him round the neck with his right, and swung him twice round like a cat. Bendy succeeded in getting the lock with his right leg, when Caunt gave him a twist, threw, and fell heavily on him, a little to the derangement of the Nottingham heroes, who shouted vociferously.

46. Caunt again succeeded in catching Bendy by the neck under his powerful arm, threw and fell heavily on him, but at the same time came with great force against the ground himself.

47. Caunt led off with the left, catching Bendy on the forehead. Bendy retreated, hit Caunt as he came in with his left on his distorted phiz, dropped, and looked up in derision. Appeal from this species of generalship seemed now to be idle, and was not repeated. [He slipped through Caunt's hands, which he was entitled to do.—ED.]

The succeeding ten rounds were fought in the same style. Little worthy of note occurred; each in turn obtaining some trifling advantage in the hitting or falling, but neither exhibited any disposition to say enough, although we thought that Bendigo, from his repeated falls, began to evince symptoms of fatigue. The confusion round the ring continued most annoying, although the ropes and stakes were still preserved entire. Many persons, from the pressure of those behind, were completely exhausted, and happy to beat a retreat. For ourselves (Ed. of *Bell's Life*), we had repeatedly to bear the weight of some half-dozen neighbours, to which the bodies of both Caunt and Bendigo were occasionally added as they fell over the ropes on us. During all this time the members of the London Ring, with one or two exceptions (Macdonald and Johnny Broome in particular), were perfectly quiescent, and looked on with modest timidity, evidently afraid to interfere with the 'club law' of the Nottingham bands, who were regularly organized, and obeyed the signals of their leaders with a discipline worthy of a better cause.

An impartial observation convinced us that Caunt's partisans quite rivalled those of Bendigo in riotous ruffianism. (Ed. *Pugilistica*.)

58. Bendigo 'jumped Jim Crow' round his man,

tipped him a left-handed smeller, and dropped without a return.

59. Caunt followed Bendy to the corner of the ring, hitting out left and right, but without precision, and certainly without doing execution. Bendy nailed him with his left in the old style, and slipped down, but instantly jumped up to renew the round. Caunt, instead of stopping to fight, considering the round over, ran across the ring to his corner, Bendy after him, till they reached the ropes, and after a confused scramble, in which Bendy used his left and right behind Caunt's back, both were down, amidst general expressions of distaste at this style of fighting, but loud applause for Bendy.

60. Caunt no sooner on his legs, than to his man, but Bendy escaped his intended compliments left and right, threw in his left on the mouth, and dropped, Caunt falling over him.

61. One hour and twenty-four minutes had now elapsed, but there were still no symptoms of an approaching termination to the battle; each appeared fresh on his pins and strong; and, although Caunt showed awful flesh wounds on his dial, there was nothing to diminish the hopes of his friends (!). Bendy exhibited but a few slight con-

tusions, and although, no doubt, shaken by the falls, and his own repeated prostrations, he appeared as active and leary as ever. Caunt, anxious to be at work, rattled to his man, hitting left and right, but Bendy retired, and fell back across the ropes.

62. Bendy again on the retreat; Caunt after him, hitting wildly and without precision left and right. Bendy gave him an upper pop with his left, and slipped down. Caunt was retiring, when Bendy jumped up again to renew active operations, but Caunt dropped on his knees, looked up in Bendy's face, grinning, as much as to say, 'Would you?' and Bendy, deeming discretion the better part of valour, contented himself with shaking his fist and retiring to his corner. Spring here remarked that jumping up to hit a man when the round was over, and when he was unprepared, was as much foul as striking a man down, and in this we perfectly concur. [No appeal was made, but the Squire sent to Clark to caution his man that such conduct was dangerous.—ED.]

63. Caunt let fly left and right, but missed his blows. Both slipped down on their knees in the struggle which followed, and laughed at each other. In Caunt's laugh, from the state of his mug, there was little of the comic.

64. Bendy renewed his hanky-panky tricks and trotted round his opponent. Caunt rushed to him, but he retreated to the ropes, hit up, and dropped, but instantly rose again to renew the round. Caunt was with him, but he again got down, falling over the bottom rope; and Caunt narrowly escaped dropping with his knee on a tender part.

65. Bendy again dropped his left on the sly on Caunt's damaged phiz, and went down. Caunt fell over him, jumped up, and retired to his corner.

66. A slight rally in which wild hits were exchanged, and Bendy received a pop in the mouth, which drew the claret. Bendy dropped on one knee, but although Caunt might have hit him in this position, he merely drew back his hand and refrained.

67. Bendy came up cautious, keeping at a distance for a few seconds, when he slyly approached, popped in a tremendous body-blow with his left, and dropped, as if from the force of his own delivery, but evidently from a desire to avoid the return. Caunt winced under the effect of this hit, and went to his corner.

68. Caunt quickly advanced to his work, but Bendy retreated to the corner, waited for him,

popped in a slight facer, and in a wild scramble got down.

69. Bendy threw in another heavy body-blow with his left, and was going down, when Caunt, with great adroitness, caught him round the neck with his left arm, lifted him completely off the ground, and holding him for a few seconds, fell heavily on him.

70—73. Scrambling rounds, in which wild exchanges took place, and Bendy slipped down as usual to avoid punishment.

74. Caunt to the charge, and Bendy on the retreat to the corner, where he succeeded in flinging in his left with terrific force on Caunt's damaged cheek, and dropped.

75. Bendy again on the retreat, till he came to the ropes, over which he was forced, Caunt on him.

76. Caunt planted his left on Bendy's pimple, and he slipped down.

77. A scrambling round in which both hit wildly and without effect. Caunt in vain tried to nail his man with his right; he was always too high, and Bendy went down. The uproar without the ring was tremendous, and whips and sticks were indiscriminately applied.

78. Bendy, after some dodging, delivered his right heavily on Caunt's body, and got down. It was a fearful smack.

79. Caunt led off with his left; Bendy ducked to avoid; and in the close both were down. Bendy was too cunning to allow his opponent the chance of the throw.

80. Bendy made his favourite sly hit with his left on Caunt's smeller, and slipped down without the account being balanced. 'Time' was very inaccurately kept, a minute instead of half that time being frequently allowed. [The blame was alternately in each corner, the seconds continuing their attentions to their men, heedless of the call of the holder of the watch.—ED.]

81. Bendy again displayed symptoms of fatigue, and was tenderly nursed. On coming to the scratch, however, he planted his left on Caunt's carcase, and slipped down.

82. Caunt led off. Bendy retreated to the ropes, and fell backwards, stopping, but instantly jumped up to recommence hostilities, when Caunt literally ran away across the ring, with his head down, Bendigo after him, hitting him in the back of his neck. At length Caunt reached his corner, and in the scramble which followed, and in which Caunt

seemed to have lost his presence of mind, both went down, amidst contemptuous shouts at the imputed pusillanimity of the Champion.

83. Bendy, on the retreat, hit up; Caunt returned the compliment on Bendy's mouth with his left, and on Bendy attempting to get down, he caught him round the neck with undiminished strength, pulled him up, threw him over, and fell heavily on him.

84. Bendy, on being lifted on his second's knee, showed blood from the mouth, and was certainly shaken by the last fall; still he came up boldly but cautiously. Caunt rattled to him left and right, but he retreated towards the stake, which Caunt caught with his right as he let fly at him, and Bendy slipped down, receiving a body-tap as he fell.

85. Caunt rushed to his man, but Bendy, on his attempting to close, got down, unwilling to risk another heavy fall. He was obviously getting fatigued from his exertions and the excessive heat of the sun.

The uproar was now greater than ever; the referee was driven into the ring, and the roaring and bawling in favour of Bendigo and in contempt of Caunt were beyond description. We (Ed.

Bell's Life) were overwhelmed again and again, and were with difficulty extracted from a pyramid of our fellow-men by the welcome aid of Jack Macdonald; our togs torn, and our tile quite shocking. The exertions of Jem Ward and others enabled them to restore the referee to his position, but he was evidently in a twitter, and the whips and sticks often reached within an inch of his 'castor,' while they fell heavily on the nobs of some of his neighbours. Several 'Corinthians,' who endeavoured to brave the storm, were involved in the general *mêlée*, and had sufficient reason to be disgusted with the conduct of the parties towards whom they are always disposed to vouchsafe their patronage, and who, as we have already said, with few exceptions looked on inactive. [These observations are coloured, and form part of the 'manipulation' undergone by the report, as revised under the suggestions and supervision of the Caunt and Spring party. The ruin of their confident hopes was impending.— ED.]

86. The Nottingham hero came up nothing daunted, but with an evident determination to continue to play the old soldier. Caunt, as usual, evinced a desire to get to his opponent, but the

latter jumped away, and waiting his opportunity threw in his left heavily on the big 'un's eye, and, in escaping from the retort, slipped down.

87. Caunt, although so repeatedly hit, came up as fresh and strong as ever (?). He was incapable, however, of parrying the cunning dodges of Bendy, who again gave him a stinging rap on the cheek, and staggering back, fell amidst cries of 'Foul,' and appeals from Caunt's friends to the referee; but in the din which prevailed no decision was obtained. [They were both fencing for 'time,' and told by the Squire to 'go on.'—Ed. *Pugilistica.*]

88. Two hours had now elapsed, and still there was no apparent approximation towards a termination of the combat, while the confusion which prevailed round the ring prevented anything like a dispassionate criticism of the operations within. Bendy came up slowly, while Caunt was evidently disposed to annihilate him, as indeed his formidable fists induced every one to believe he would have done long before; but Bendy prudently kept out of distance until a slight opening in the guard of Caunt enabled him to jump in and deliver his left twice in succession, on effecting which he slipped down, and looked up with a triumphant leer at the mystified Champion.

89. Bendy again made himself up for mischief, and cleverly avoiding Caunt's attempt to reach him left and right, delivered a heavy hit with his right on the Champion's ribs, which was distinctly heard amidst the row; after which he dropped, and Caunt retired to the corner.

90. A close, and struggle for the fall, which Caunt easily obtained, falling heavily on his adversary, and his knee again happily escaped pressure on a vital part. From Bendy's shifty tactics, it was impossible for Caunt to avoid falling as he did. It, however, led to a fresh appeal by Johnny Hannan, on the part of Bendigo, and a contradiction by Molineaux on the part of Caunt. The umpires disagreed, and the question having been put to the referee, amidst a horrible outcry raised by both parties, he decided 'Fair!' declaring that there was nothing intentional on the part of Caunt.

91. A scrambling round. A close in which, after having delivered his left, Bendy contrived to get down, amidst fresh cries of 'Foul!' 'Fair!'

92. Exchanges of hits with the left, when Bendy, stooping to avoid the repetition of Caunt's blow, as he was going down, struck Caunt below the waistband and near the bottom of his stomach. Bendy fell on his back at the moment, while

Caunt dropped his hands upon the place affected, and fell as if in great pain. An indescribable scene of turmoil ensued; shouts of 'Foul!' and 'Fair!' escaped from 'a thousand tongues—a thousand pair of iron lungs,' many evidently influenced by their desires and not their convictions. There is no doubt that the blow, according to the rules of the Ring, was foul; but that it was intentional we cannot say, as it was struck when Bendy was in the act of falling. At last the umpires, disagreeing, made the customary appeal to the referee, who, almost deafened by the roaring of the multitude, finally said he had not seen the blow, and consequently could not pronounce it foul. The seconds immediately returned to their principals, and the latter, time being called, commenced the

93rd, and last round. The men were quickly at the scratch, and Caunt commenced operating left and right, catching Bendy slightly on the forehead. Bendigo was forced back upon the ropes, almost in a recumbent position, but got up and was again knocked down, and Caunt turned from him, considering the round had concluded. Bendy, however, awake to every chance of administering punishment, jumped up as he had done before, and rushing after Caunt, who was half turned from him, was about to let fly, when Caunt dropped on his nether end, evidently disinclined to renew or continue that round. And now a final, and, as it turned out, a decisive appeal was made to the referee (not by the umpires, but by Jem Ward, Hannan, and others), who, with very little hesitation, pronounced the fatal word 'Foul!' declaring that he considered Caunt had deliberately violated the rules of the Ring by going down without a blow, and had therefore lost the fight."

If the number of times Bendigo went down "to avoid punishment" be considered, the verdict must be regarded as an astounding one—only to be accounted for by the intimidation of the Nottingham "Lambs!"

The extent to which a well-supported encouragement of bruising—whether with the gloves or naked fists—may benefit this country in the future is hardly to be over-estimated. It has already done much to lift John Bull into his present position, and any extensive resort to cowardly weapons, such as the dagger, the knife, or the stiletto, can only be regarded as a very bad sign of the times. I have elsewhere expressed my opinion of that miserable weapon the sword-stick, and therefore will not go any further into the question, which is really out of place in a boxing book; still the natural disgust one feels at the indiscriminate use of cold steel, prompts me to give the following from the *Daily Telegraph*, so late as August 9, 1897—

"Within the past fortnight no fewer than nine charges of assault involving the use of the knife have been brought before magistrates sitting in the various London districts. In two or three cases jealousy was the avowed incentive, but in nearly all the others they were the outcome of street frays, and though with one or two exceptions no fatal result is anticipated, there can, according to the evidence adduced, be but little doubt that at the moment when the attacks were made, although actual murder may not have been in the mind of the individual whose hand directed the blade, he was reckless as to what the result might be.

"Of course it is impossible to say with any degree of certainty to what this undesirable development of a passion for blood-spilling among the rougher members of the community is attributable, but it is just possible that bad example of foreign importation may have something to do with it. At the present time the Italian colony in Clerkenwell is full to overflowing, and at the East-end of London there appears to be no abatement in the periodical arrival of alien nondescripts that reckon amongst their number not a few who, in their own country, are accustomed to carry a sharp-edged weapon for other purposes than to carve bread and cheese. As regards the natives of the sunny South who congregate thick almost as bees in a hive in the courts and alleys of Eyre Street Hill and Leather Lane, and whose benevolent mission it is to make London life depressed by August heat more endurable by means of ice-creams, now it is high tide of business with them, and in the abounding dirty little beer-shops of the locality there are nightly quarrels and fights, and 'cold steel' is not uncommonly exhibited, if not actually used, by the heated disputants. Such suggestions of sanguinary conflict cannot have a wholesome effect on the minds of those who are there to see what the row is about. As a rule, even the most ill-conditioned of our own lower-class population are dead set against stabbing and stabbers. Exasperated to show fight, they make fists at the foe, and rely on them to compel him to knuckle under, but familiarized to the sight of the knife drawn in settlement of street quarrels it may make all the difference.

"It is a public danger more difficult to put a stop to than that introduced by the cheap revolver. To place that mischievous weapon out of reach of silly youths and crack-brained adults requires but a simple alteration of existing law, but a pocket-knife is as commonly carried about as a pocket-handkerchief, and its murderous misuse cannot be guarded against, except by dealing with offenders with severity. Sudden fury and instantaneous impulse cannot be pleaded when a clasp-knife is brought into felonious use. A lusty blow with a stick or with a missile snatched up and thrown admits, perhaps, of some excuse, but there is little or none in the other case. The weapon has to be sought for and opened before it can be used, so that the cowardly crime cannot be without deliberate intent.

"As already stated, in most of the cases alluded to mere maiming has been the worst that has resulted; but in at least one instance a clasp-knife assault has ended tragically. At Worship Street Police Court on Saturday, a young Polish Jew, named Lewis Lewinsky, was brought up on remand. The previous charge against him was one of cutting and wounding; but since then the matter has assumed a graver complexion, the unfortunate victim having died in hospital. It appeared in evidence that about a fortnight since Lewinsky, whose age is nineteen, in company with other young roughs residing in that notorious locality, Dorset Street, Spitalfields, were 'larking' and interfering with two old people who chanced to be coming that way. A man named Meady remonstrated with them, and compelled them to desist, at which the accused lad Lewinsky took offence, and was impudent to Meady, who, it is alleged, made an attempt to kick him. A friend of Lewinsky was standing near, eating his dinner of bread and meat with a clasp-knife, and this latter accused snatched away from him, and, turning on Meady, threatened to stick it into him. The quarrel, however, ceased for a time. About two hours after Lewinsky again met Meady, and it appeared that meantime he had not parted with the borrowed knife. He had it in his hand when the altercation recommenced, and the two had a struggle together and rolled on the ground. Meady presently scrambled to his feet, and, with his hand pressed against his left side, exclaimed, 'I've got it.' He was conveyed to the London Hospital, where his dying deposition was taken in presence of a magistrate. On that occasion prisoner was taken to the bedside, and, pointing towards him, Meady remarked, 'That's the man who did it,' and shortly afterwards the man died of the injury inflicted on him. The charge on which Lewinsky is again remanded is that of feloniously killing and slaying."

Gangs of roughs have recently made certain highways almost impossible for decent people, but these are the kicking, violent roughs who are usually bent on plunder of some sort, and they are not "knifers" as a rule. What will happen if the pocket-knife is brought into general requisition?

If attacked and compelled to defend your life or your property, never hesitate to use your best endeavours to disable the assailant. It is no use being kind and considerate on such occasions. The rough will not mind fatally injuring you, so always go for a vital part, and hit hard. If you get him down don't let any squeamish, sentimental nonsense prevent your knocking out his brains with half a brick, should such be lying handy. He is a pest to society, and must be treated as such. I know, from experience, that much may be done by hard and well-directed hitting, and by activity, but it is well to remember that, when you have repulsed the attack satisfactorily, a change of locality is desirable. You never know to what extent accomplices may be lurking in the neighbourhood. A good thick stick is the first rampart, then come the fists, and then, as a *dernier ressort*, a clean pair of heels.

CHAPTER XIII.

WEAK POINTS AND DANGEROUS HITS.

THOUGH it is seldom that permanent or fatal injuries result from fights, it is right to become thoroughly well acquainted with anatomy up to the point of knowing where to "go for," and where to protect yourself.

Between the crown of your head and the line of your belt there are certain places which it must be your constant care to protect, either by dodging or guarding.

In the old days of the Ring the eyes were very important, because, in long fights, they were often shut in by the folds of swollen and bruised skin which were produced by repeated visitations from the adversary's knuckles. This was most noticeable in many of Tom Sayers' fights—so much so that it almost looks as though the gallant little Champion relied on blinding his opponents before finishing them off! In the present day the eyes cannot be called weak points, because the gloves, even when of small size, to a great extent prevent the bruising which was formerly brought about by the bare knuckles.

The sides and whole of the lower portions of the head, including the temples and ears, and more particularly the jaw, are all weak points. The throat, between the jaw and the collar-bones, is much shielded by the chin, otherwise it, too, must be looked upon as a weak point. The upper portions of the chest are so beautifully protected by the double arch of the ribs and by the breast-bone, that blows do not often do much damage in these regions, though bad hits may be given rather high up under the arms.

It is when we get lower down that danger is to be apprehended. It is that zone or girdle, about eight inches in width, which extends all round the body. In depth it may roughly be measured from the mark, just where the ribs divide, and a point on the belt vertically below the mark. Two lines carried on horizontal planes through these points and right round the body will include all the more dangerous body-hits. The "mark," "short ribs," and "kidney hit," all fall within these limits.

In "dangerous hits" are not included those accidents which will sometimes occur in the ring, such as injuries on the stakes, etc., but only those hits which when they get well home are likely to occasion considerable damage and pain.

First and foremost in the list stands out the celebrated "pint o-the-jaw" hit, which is answerable for sending more men to sleep than all the others put together. Here we have a fine example of mechanical advantage. From the point of the jaw to the point where the cervical vertebra joins the skull, the lower jaw helps to form a lever of several inches in length, and it is easily seen that a small force applied at the chin end of the lever will bring about a twist of the head in the direction of the blow. Flush hits in the "middle of the face," as they used to say in the old accounts, are at times trying to put up with, but they are as nothing when compared to hits of equal force on the point of the jaw. There is not the same head-jerking sensation, and you are not shaken to the same extent. A hit upwards on the jaw is bad, for, if hard enough, it will lift you off your feet and deposit you on the ground, but it is the *sideway* hit which is the worst of all.

Here is another example of a wonderful provision of nature. In our ordinary movements we are more *likely* to strike the *front* of our faces, so the forehead is made particularly strong and thick, and, just above the eyes, there are two layers of bone to be broken through before the brain can be reached. At the back, too, the skull is thick, to resist falls, etc.; but on the sides the necessity does not so much exist, since in ordinary falls the sides of the head are protected by the shoulders. All this points to the desirability of getting at the side of the head and jaw whenever practicable.

The next most dangerous hit is that on the "mark," which, as most of my readers are aware, is synonymous to "pit of the stomach," and to the "bread-basket" or "commissariat department" of ring-side phraseology. This spot, only about the size of a penny-piece, seems to be a very centre of nerves, for a slight prod with the end of a stick in the exact place will cause most people to double up. Being well above the belt, this locality is the mark for your fists—a sort of bull's-eye always to be aimed for.

One of the chief reasons for not letting the hands drop below the belt is that the arms may always be "there or thereabouts" when the mark is assailed, and, according to our present notions,

WEAK POINTS AND DANGEROUS HITS. 257

it seems well to have the "thick" of the right fore-arm nearly always laid across the mark and in actual contact with the body.

When hitting at the mark let the blow be well driven home, so as to make itself properly felt: when protecting yourself from a similar visitation, tighten the muscles of the abdomen, tuck in the "innards," and keep the arm firmly across the dangerous spot, for by this means most of the mischief will be taken out of the blow. A good many people have been killed, from time to time, by these hits, and this is why so much preference should be given to guarding or avoiding body-blows.

The "short ribs," on both sides of the body, just above the belt, are very apt to suffer from contracted arm-hits at close quarters; and further round, on either side of the spine, lie the kidneys, which may be seriously damaged by blows in their immediate neighbourhood, if delivered with the naked fist. So that, speaking generally, you have to consider the zone round the body just above the belt: amongst boxers it might aptly be termed the "dangerous zone."

It is true that men have from time to time been killed in fights with the fists and gloves;

in such cases death is very often due to some natural weakness more than to the actual hit itself. Thus a man with a weak heart may die sooner than he otherwise would through the excitement of a protracted fight.

It seems improbable in the highest degree that pugilism, even carried to the extent of prize-fighting, really shortens life. Take the following ages of ten celebrated prize-fighters of the older school—all men who took their share of punishment and fought many well-contested battles:— John Broughton, sometimes alluded to as the "Father of British Boxing," reached the age of 85; Dan Mendoza was 73; "Mr." John Jackson was 76; Tom Belcher was 71; John Gully, 81; Tom Cribb, 67; Jem Ward, 82; William Thompson ("Bendigo"), 69; William Perry ("the Tipton Slasher"), 61; and Ben Caunt was 46 when he died. This gives the respectable average of 71.1 years, and it must be remembered that in some cases, *e.g.* Caunt and Perry—death was traceable to causes quite outside the work of the Ring, in one case pneumonia, and the other case free living having brought about the end.

Poor Tom Sayers departed this life at the early age of 38; he died of consumption, and it is said that his rather rapid decline was accelerated by dissipation; certain it is that his death was in no way attributable to the many hard knocks he received and gave during the course of his brilliant career.

CHAPTER XIV.

NATURAL FIGHTERS.

THESE dreadful specimens are like poets —born, not made. They spring into existence having either spurned all offers of instruction, or having never been in the way of learning. As hinted elsewhere, it is well to "take on" these men as often as possible—they will so completely illustrate and bring home to you the truth of the saying that the "unexpected happens." As a rule they are strong men who have been lucky in polishing off a few weaker men in a rural district, or poor little milliners' assistants in a town. They are only dangerous on account of their violence and rushing propensities, and it is your game to turn all this expenditure of energy to your own account.

I remember once being pressed to spar with a man of this class. It was after a dinner in the

SLIPPING.

summer time, and I felt quite pleased to think that we were to fight on a big lawn with lots of room to get about. He was two or three stone heavier than myself, and had a "local" name, so of course it was a question of defensive tactics at first. In the first two rushes he came on like a tiger, and must have hit out twenty times with both hands in these and the following rounds. Needless to say, I was obliged to retreat, and did so, as slowly as possible, using the weaving guards with both arms and completely escaping punishment. In getting away I noticed that his hands seemed very high; and that it would be possible to get under his guard without much difficulty. With this idea in view I waited for his next rush, and standing quite firm met him with a perfectly straight hit flush in the face with my left. It was my one and only hit; the gentleman retired with some mumbled remarks about hard hitting. He had really hurled himself against my fist, and himself contributed by far the largest share of his punishment.

This is the best way to treat a rusher, only you should not do it until you know fairly well what he intends to do, and then, if you are sufficiently heavy, stand quite firm, and, leaning forward in his direction, hit out as straight as possible.

So much depends on the relative strength and weight of any two men. It is very difficult for a man who is *greatly* inferior in weight to do much against a powerful rusher. Of course, if he cannot keep him at a distance, either by countering or retreating, there is the chance of a strangling match, in which the bigger man will win. When a little fellow is caught in this way he may be swung around, scragged, cross-buttocked, or punched into insensibility, and then dropped limp and helpless on the ground. In such circumstances science won't help you much; if you are hopelessly small and weak and have only nature's weapons you can do but little in such a case.

William Perry, "the Tipton Slasher," twice met the gigantic Yankee, Charles Freeman, towards the end of December 1842, and here the disparity was very considerable, the Giant scaling 18st. 12lbs., against the Slasher's 13st. odd. Still here the smaller man had plenty of weight behind his blows, and of course Freeman could not be looked upon as a boxer of any class. The first fight was interrupted, and the second was very properly given against Perry, who had repeatedly gone down without being hit. Freeman was a perfect Hercules, only a little under seven feet, and very well proportioned, so that he was not an easy man to "get at," and his opponent resorted to the shifty methods of dropping to avoid punishment as his only chance. As it turned out, this policy lost him the fight.

As you go down in the weights from "lights" to "feathers," and from "feathers" to "bantams," you approach a limit, it may be the 4st. infant, who could not possibly damage any ordinary man's frame, if allowed to hit at it all day long.

Thus we see that two *very* light weights may pound each other for ever so long without any alarming results. Two heavy weights cannot do this with impunity, and the reason is not far to seek.

The general strength of the bones, cartilages, etc., in the heads and faces of men of all weights is much the same. The bones in the frame of a big man are not so very much stronger than those in a very much smaller individual. A small man's teeth are just as strongly fixed in as a giant's, but the punching power or *momentum* is very different in the two cases.

Suppose M represents the mass or quantity of blood, bones, and flesh of any particular man. The quantity of *material*, so to speak; then if f

represents the acceleration of his hit, the force of his blow may be fairly represented by the *product* of these two factors—*i.e.* by Mf—at the moment of contact.

It will easily be seen that if M be very considerably diminished, as in the case of a very light man, and f very slightly increased, for the light man is supposed to hit quicker, and that if M' and f' be taken to represent the factors in the second case, we may easily conceive that Mf might be much greater than $M'f'$.

To fight with any sort of success against rough and heavy natural fighters, you must have a respectable share of weight, say 10st. 7lbs. at the very least.

CHAPTER XV.

COMPARISONS AND QUALIFICATIONS.

WHEN confronted with questions of complexity it is often the safer plan to leave them alone and say nothing, so that possibly some of my readers will think that this chapter should not have been written. As a rule we have insufficient data when attempting to decide the comparative merits of any two boxers or fighters. Still I am of opinion that by carefully looking into various contests one may to some extent follow the general ideas, tactics, and methods of any particular man, and at any rate gain some information and instruction by the effort. Thus if we follow, say, Nat Langham's career, we find that he was a wonderful believer in the straight, ever ready, left hand, which was always popping in at the right moment for him and the wrong moment for the other man: we also find that his right was rarely used except for short work at close quarters, and that it was then very effective in the short, true, contracted arm hits. It is not to be supposed that Langham would ever have defeated the gallant Tom Sayers had it not been for his wonderfully true hitting powers, and, though the fighters of to-day may look down upon the old-time men as deficient in leg work, they must be reminded that straight hitting of the best description is difficult to get round—certain it is that the old fighters were well plucked 'uns and could take much punishment without flinching.

Then again there was Jem Mace, probably the most scientific glove-fighter of the old school, whose position and style were almost faultless. It is not very hard, in reading through the accounts of his chief contests, to detect where his science befriended him. A straight hard hitter, good with both hands, *creber utraque manu*, and particularly easy in his methods of breaking ground and in the rapidity of his leg work. One would, of course, have a better chance of forming sound opinions if one could actually see the old contests reproduced by the processes of moving photographs, but we have to be content with accounts which, though old, may be taken as fairly correct.

Examine the more modern fights and go through them with care. Do we not find all the peculiarities of the men bearing with special force on their various contests? The rather rigid strength of Jem Smith, the nippiness or nimbleness of Charlie Mitchell, the various points of excellence in men like J. L. Sullivan, Jake Kilrain, Peter Jackson, F. P. Slavin, James J. Corbett and Bob Fitzsimmons, all come out in every fight, and the comparison frequently narrows itself down to a question of *condition*.

A very first-rate man in bad condition will often beat another of inferior science though in the pink of training, and an unlucky blow may polish off the best man, and this is why it is so hard, after witnessing a few fights, to form a just conclusion.

If, then, it is so difficult to arrive at satisfactory conclusions in the matter of comparative merit amongst living men, how much harder must it be to say what these same men would or would not do if they could be confronted with the heroes of the past?

Soon after his victory over Corbett the question was put to Fitzsimmons—" How much of a showing, if any, would such men as Jem Mace, Tom Sayers, Bob Brettle, Tom King, and other fighters of their time be able to make against men in your class?" The plucky middle weight is reported to have replied:—"The answer to your question is necessarily brief. In the first place, none of those men possessed the leg qualities common to-day among prize-fighters. The one object with them was to smash a man in the eyes, closing them up so as to blind him. They also played havoc with the stomach. They went at it with a ferocity that was brutal, and seldom showed much skill in boxing. Frequently they broke each other's arms. To tell the truth, I do not think they realized that the jaw was the vital point. If they did, they took no advantage of that knowledge, and only put their men out by hammering them into insensibility. They used to fight hours at a stretch and went at it rough and tumble at the same time. Now, to come to a comparison between them and myself, or any other fighter in my class. If I was pitted against one of those men I would simply go at him with the science and hitting powers I possess, and put him out, perhaps in the first round. With all their strength and courage a stiff punch on the chin would send them to sleep just as easily as though they were school-boys. They would have no more chance than an amateur, and it would be an easy job to literally smash one of them all up. Those men fought like tigers, and hit wherever they could, while the modern fighter uses science, places his blows where they will do the most good, and accomplishes the same end in one-tenth the time, and almost invariably without bloodshed. They were game fellows, but to-day would not be in it. Most any fighter would agree with me in this matter."

Very possibly modern fighters might agree with this, but, even if science has made such a forward step in the matter of leg work and "pint-o'-the-jaw 'its," it seems hardly fair to allude to the above-named old fighters as a set of ferocious old savages who smashed one another till one or other or both fell down from sheer exhaustion! Jem Mace would not like to be so described, and neither he nor Tom Sayers could have been particularly easy men for any one to get at.

I don't wish to be misunderstood, or for a moment to say that the best and most scientific modern fighter could *not* defeat any or all of the old Champions, but I do say that until two men have actually fought together there is no certainty about the result. A good left like Nat Langham's takes some getting over, and the punching would hardly be all on one side with opponents like Mace, Sayers, Brettle, or King.

According to the above quotation, Fitzsimmons admits that the old champions "also played havoc with the stomach." Precisely. They *did*, and, I believe, would again do so if they could be brought to life. It was by playing this havoc with the "commissariat" that Fitzsimmons himself snatched the Championship from Corbett, and, to that extent, copied the old timers!

We can never at any moment say for certain that we have seen the best man the world will ever produce. Records are always being broken as regards times of races, heights and lengths of jumps, cricket scores, etc., etc., and we cannot say that what we have reached will *never* be exceeded. In the case of pugilists we are still more at sea, for we cannot put anything to the test because there must always be two men, and one, being in his grave, cannot toe the scratch. The great Mr. Jackson—I refer to the very superior and well-patronized person who lived and taught at the latter end of last century—was a good man, and probably thought himself better than any who had been before or could come after him, and yet his coloured namesake Peter, of the present day, would probably be far more than his match. It is perhaps only human nature for any "Champion of the World" to think that he is the Admirable Crichton, and has reached the summit of human possibilities. The Senior Wrangler may think the same, but if his Tripos is in a bad year, he may be really inferior to the fifth Wrangler in an exceptionally good year—the two never join issue or try conclusions, and therefore never know for certain.

So that, as regards comparative merit between boxers of different times, we can only say *now* that, as far as we can see, science has advanced— has advanced with the popularity of the Art, and that a first-rate man to-day would, weights, condition, age, height, etc., being equal, defeat a first-rate man of sixty years ago. To go further than this appears to me presumptuous.

But to abandon this speculative digression, and come back to facts, it seems probable that health and general *condition* play the largest part in those conflicts where Dame Fortune has smiled on a previously defeated competitor : but we must go yet further in looking for the reasons for these reversals.

A beats B; B beats C; C beats D; D beats E.

Now it would appear to the superficial observer that A should certainly beat E. It has, however, been shown over and over again that E will occasionally beat A, and this without any marked falling off in A's style, condition, or strength. The reason is probably this:—E has some peculiarity of style or tactics which A has not been accustomed to in the course of his practice. B probably fought *as he expected him to fight*, and therefore he beat him; then E comes along, the unexpected happens, A gets flurried and thrown out and ultimately disappoints his backers.

Similarly good fencers, accustomed to the recognized usages and style of "the school," have been "pinked" by novices who opened in unexpected and unorthodox fashion, and fine exhibition sparrers get knocked all of a heap by roughs who don't play the legitimate game.

All this points to the necessity, elsewhere emphasized in these pages, of accustoming yourself to the fighting habits of all sorts and conditions of men—for your experience cannot be too widely extended.

You will never find a correct principle tripping, but you will notice how often you fail yourself in correct application.

On January 28, 1862, Jem Mace met and defeated Tom King, a man who stood many inches over him, and pulled down the beam at 12st. 8lbs., whilst his own weight was given at the middle-weight limit. With regard to this fight, the comment at the time was that Mace's superiority as a scientific pugilist alone enabled him to contend with and finally defeat his brave, powerful, and, in size and physique, formidable antagonist.

The two fights are given below, because a study of them both is instructive as showing how the fortune of war favoured first one and then the other of two men undeniably in the first rank of pugilists of the day.

MACE v. KING.

"*Round* 1. Having gone through the customary friendly salutation at the scratch, each man drew back and threw himself into position. There was at this moment a silence that might be felt, and the eager glances directed by all towards the combatants evinced the interest with which every movement was being watched by those surrounding the ring. There was undoubtedly much to rivet the attention of the patrons of the art, for though both were unquestionably fine fellows, yet there was that disparity between them which could not fail to impress itself even on the uninitiated. Mark the towering height of King, standing a clear 6ft. 2in. in his stockings, and, as he faces his opponent with attentive watchfulness, but without a sign of nervousness or anxiety, how immense and preponderating appear the advantages in his favour! Tom, we were informed by Langham, when he last scaled, pulled down 12st. 8lbs., and taken for all in all must be declared a model man, although some judges of athletes declared his loins too slender for a man of his height. Tom, like Mace, has a bright, keen eye, but he lacks the square-cut jaw-bone and hard angular contour which some judges of 'points' declare to be always found in the 'thoroughbred' boxer. Be that as it may, King's length of reach, firm, round muscle, skin ruddy with the glow of health, and cheerful, courageous aspect gave promise of a formidable opponent, even to the scientific champion, Jem Mace. As to the Champion, who pulled down 11st. 4lbs. on the preceding Monday, he was 'all there,' and, as he himself said, felt 'fit as a fiddle.' After keeping on guard a few seconds, during which Mace was keenly scrutinizing him, Tom dropped his hands, resting his left upon his left thigh; Jem, being out of range, and seeing that Tom had lowered his daddles, followed suit, and the position of the pair at this moment caused some astonishment. Tom rubbed his left forearm with his right hand, and Jem, who also felt the chilly effects of the morning air on coming out of his flannels, rubbed his breast with his right palm. Tom, in shifting, had got nearer to his own corner, when Jem advanced, and, from the manner he gathered himself together, evidently intended mischief; his left was admirably poised, while his right played with firm elasticity, ready as a guard, or, if occasion presented itself, a shoot. Tom, however, was on the alert, and Mace, after putting out a feeler or two, sprung back to tempt Tom to follow. King, who at first seemed a little puzzled, smiled and retreated, cool as a cucumber in an ice-well. There was more than one repetition of the movement we have here described, these men shifting, changing position, and manœuvring all over the ring, without coming to business. King had heard so much of the ability of Mace that he felt he was standing before the best tactician of the day, and would not lead off. Mace, on the other hand, with the perception of a practised general, found that he had before him a dangerous and determined antagonist; one whom it would not do to treat in the style he had made an example of big Sam Hurst. At length, after a display of almost every sort of drawing and defensive tactics, Mace got well in, delivering a neat nobber with the left, stopping the return, and getting away. King dashed at him, his height enabling him to hit over Jem's guard, and Tom got one in on Mace's head with the right; the men closed and fibbed, then getting on to the ropes both went down. The seconds were instant in their attendance, Bos Tylor claiming 'first blood' for King, which was admitted, as the cochineal was trickling from a cut on the Champion's chin. King's partisans were in ecstasies, and 'Who'll lay two to one now?' met no response.

2. The cold rain now came down in earnest, and did not much abate throughout the rest of the mill. With ready alacrity each man came from his corner and scratched simultaneously with his opponent. Mace, who was still bleeding, looked flushed. After a little sparring, Mace popped in his left. His second hit was prettily countered,

but notwithstanding King's length, Jem's blow seemed hardest, reaching home a 'thought' before his adversary's poke. Another exchange, Tom getting on the side of Mace's head, but not severely, and Jem's smack in return sounding all round the ring. In the close both were down.

3. The ball had now been fairly opened, and each bout improved the spirit of the performance, on which even the pitiless rain could not throw a damper. Jem, on coming from his corner, was still distilling the *elixir vitæ* from the old spot, which as yet seemed the only mark made. King went dashing in to force the fighting, and the hot haste of the onslaught marred the pretty position of Jem. Tom, who seemed to hit from the forearm rather than the shoulder, got home his left on the jaw, and then, with the right, reached Jem's head; his superiority of length of reach being fully demonstrated. Jem, however, quite balanced accounts by two severe props in the nob; King closed, and Mace got down.

4. The rapidity of King's fighting seemed somewhat to surprise Mace, and he moved right and left in front of his man, his points well covered. Tom dashed in left and right, and went to work, his counsel advising the forcing principle; King, in

hitting out, had his left hand partially open; Mace cross-countered with the left a smasher, but a second attempt passed over King's shoulder. Jem broke away, and in retreating got to the centre stake. Tom, following, dashed out his right, when Mace ducked his head and slipped down, thereby escaping a rasper.

5. Mace first to scratch, King promptly facing him. As Tom tried to lead off with the left, Mace showed how well he was fortified by his left-hand guard, and then retaliating with the right, King in turn retreated. Tom, in shifting, got to the ropes, when Jem weaved in, getting both hands on head and body. Tom lashed out both hands defensively, but could not keep Jem off until he chose to retire to his own corner, where he got cleverly out of difficulty and was down.

6. King had evidently got home at the close of the last round, for Jem came up with his proboscis tinted with the carmine. Tom dashed at his man with more determination than judgment, hit from the fore-arm without doing execution; Jem, hitting up as he made the backward break, gave master Tom a straightener, who, persevering, got his man down at the ropes: no harm done.

7. Jem advanced to the scratch with a firm step

and determined bearing, as if the difficulties of his position had only produced a concentration of the resolute 'I will.' The men stood eyeing each other in the pelting rain; Jem rubbed his chest, which had a large red mark as though a warm plaster had recently been removed. After manœuvring round the ring, Mace got to range, delivering a well-aimed shot on King's cranium. As Jem broke ground he nearly lost his equilibrium from the slipperiness of the grass, but quickly steadied himself. After a feint or two they got well together and countered splendidly, Mace sending home his left on Tom's right cheek, King getting his right on the Champion's left peeper, raising a small bump, and causing him to blink like an owl in sunshine. The men, with mutual action, broke away and manœuvred all over the ring. At last Jem, measuring his man accurately, gave him such a left-hander on the snuff-box that *claret du premier crû* was copiously uncorked. As Mace retreated after this smack, Tom went in rather wildly, and closing, got his left leg between Mace's and threw him. (Cheers for King.)

8. Tom no sooner faced his man than he made play, and got his right arm round Mace; he then tried to lift him by main strength for a throw, but

the Champion put on the head-stop, with his hand on Tom's face, and King had to let him go down an easy fall.

9. King, by the advice of his seconds, again forced the fighting, slung out both hands, and closed, when Mace cleverly put on the back-heel, and down went Tom undermost.

10—14. The ropes had now got slack, and Puggy White busied himself in driving the stakes deeper, and tightening them. In this and the following four rounds, King still led off, and though his hits did not seem severe, he had got so often on Jem's eye and nose, that his friends were confident of his pulling through.

15. The odds seemed melting away like butter in the sun, and the backers of the Champion were just becoming 'knights of the rueful countenance;' while Tom's partisans were as merry and chirpy as crickets; Jerry Noon, especially, dispensing an unusual and unseemly store of chaff among the despondent patrons of Mace. King once again went at his man, and both went down at the ropes. King's seconds claimed the battle for a 'foul,' alleging that Mace had tried to force his fingers into King's eye in the struggle at the ropes; the referee crossed the ring to caution

Mace, who indignantly denied any intention of so unmanly an action.

16. King seemed determined to lose no time. He rattled in, and Mace, nothing loth, stood up and hit with him, certainly straightest and swiftest. In the close both were down at the ropes.

17. In sparring, the combatants changed positions, and paused in the centre of the ring. King had been fighting very fast and wanted a breathing time. On resuming he went in, and after some exchanges Mace got down easy at the ropes.

18. Sharp exchanges, left and right, on the cheek, mouth, and jaw, when Jem in shifting, slipped down. His seconds ran to him, but he motioned them away, resumed his perpendicular, and beckoned Tom with a smile to renew the bout. The challenge was cheerfully accepted, and fighting into a close, both were down.

19. The men were admirably seconded in both corners, and both came up clean and smiling, though each had the contour of his countenance seriously altered by his opponent's handiwork. In a close both fibbed away merrily, and both were down.

20. There was an objection by Jerry Noon that Mace had some 'foreign substance' in his left hand. King opened his hands before the referee,

and Mace, following his example, merely showed a small piece of paper in his palm, which, however, he threw away. Mace's left hand seemed somewhat puffed, and Tom's leading counsel, observing this, told King that his adversary's 'left was gone,' which it was not, for Mace, this time, took the initiative, and landed the left sharply on Tom's cheek. As Mace broke ground Tom followed, and when near the stake he landed a round hit from the right on Jem's left jaw that sent him to grass —a clean knock-down blow.

21. Tom, eager to be at work, went in, but he did not take much by his motion; after several exchanges Jem retreated. Mace slipped and got between King's legs in a defenceless position, holding himself up by the handkerchief round Tom's waist. King gallantly withheld his hand, threw up his arms and smiled, walking to his corner amidst general cheering.

22. King was now the favourite, odds being offered on him of 6 to 4, but no takers. King as before began the business, and Mace was down to close the round.

23. This was a harmless bout, King bored in; Mace missed as he retreated, backed on to the ropes, and got down.

24. Both men came up with alacrity, despite the pelting rain which streamed down their faces and limbs. King was evidently slower, and Mace tried a lead. He did not, however, get quite near enough, and Tom pursued him round the ring until both were down, Mace undermost.

25. A curious round. Tom dashed at Mace, who stopped him, then twisted round and got away. Tom followed, and Mace propped him; at the ropes, when down, both men patted each other in a good-tempered manner.

26. Mace came up determinedly, but exhibited ugly punishment on the left eye and mouth. Still he was steady, and met Tom's onslaught cleverly. King closed and tried to hold up Mace, but he slipped through his hands.

27. Tom administered a right-hander on the jaw, and down went Mace against his will for the second time.

28. Mace recovered from the effects of his floorer in an amazing manner. Tom had now a serious bump on his right eye the size of a walnut, and had otherwise lost his facial symmetry. His friends were, however, more sanguine, and urged him to keep his man at it. Tom tried to do so, but got nothing at it, and in the fall hit the stake.

29. King got a round right-hander on Mace's back of his head, and both were down—a side fall.

30. Mace seemed wonderfully steady, and in good form. King, as before, made play: the ground was so soddened, cut up and pasty, that a good foothold was impossible. Tom sent in his right, and Jem, with well-judged precision, returned with both mauleys, when King embraced him, but Mace put up the back-heel, and threw Tom cleverly on his back; as Mace rose first from the ground he patted King in a good-tempered manner, amidst cries of 'Bravo, Mace!'

31. King, as he sat on his second's knee, seemed much distressed. His sides heaved like a forge-bellows; his seconds were most assiduous, and sent him up clean and fresh. Tom came slowly from his corner; not so Jem, who advanced quickly to the scratch, and then tried to entice his man to lead off. At last he did so, and gave King as good as he sent, when Tom forced Mace to the ropes. The latter turned himself round, reversing their positions, and, after a short wrestle, threw Tom with the back-heel, a fair fall.

32. Exchanges; King on the body, Mace on the head, and both down.

33. King still forcing the fighting; Mace as

lively as a grasshopper. After some pretty exchanges, Mace got home the left on his opponent's right cheek—a cutter—a close, some fibbing, and both down, King over the lower rope and partly out of the ring.

34. Mace first from his corner, but had not long to wait for his opponent. Tom hit out with better intention than judgment, and failed to do execution. A close, Mace again got King with the back-heel, and threw him heavily.

35. The sun of success was brightening in the east, though the clouds were pouring heavily. King was suffering from his protracted exertions, and 'bellows to mend' was the case in his corner. His heart was good, and he fought gallantly into a close, catching pepper; Mace, after delivering a flush hit, falling in the middle of the ring.

36. After a little manœuvring, the men got on the ropes, when King slipped down by a pure accident. As King's friends had objected to Mace's style of getting down, there were derisive counter-cheers and cries of 'Foul!' followed by enthusiastic cheers for both men.

37. Tom's seconds found that their plan of forcing the fighting had miscarried, and now gave opposite advice. King waited for Mace, who manœuvred

and feinted, until Tom let go his left, and was countered artistically. Mace then stepped in and delivered his left full in King's dial, and in the exchange both were down in the middle of the ring.

38—40. King, finding Mace his master at outfighting, resumed his plan of going to work just as he was getting second wind. The rounds again were of the old pattern; King got the larger and heavier share of the hitting, and both were down, Mace choosing his own time to end the round. In the fortieth round King complained of Mace using him unfairly, but the referee saw nothing calling for his notice.

41, 42, 43, and last.—King was visibly distressed in the first two of these three final rounds. In the last of these bouts the combatants closed in the middle of the ring, when Mace, who had delivered a heavy thwack on King's neck, struggled with him for the fall. In going down King, who was undermost, struck the front of his head with great force on the ground. Tom's seconds had him in his corner in an instant, as the position was critical. The die was, however, cast. 'Time!' was called in vain. Mace, who was eagerly watching his opponent's corner, advanced to the scratch. The referee entered the ring, watch in hand. The eight seconds were counted; but King was still deaf to the call of 'Time!' and Mace was hailed the winner, after one hour and eight minutes of rapid fighting on both sides. Scarcely had the fiat gone forth, when a posse of police made their appearance, who, to do them justice, seemed glad that the affair was over before their arrival."

After this the majority of people held the opinion that Mace was altogether too good and scientific for King, but King himself was not of that opinion, and how the tables were turned is set forth in the following account of the return fight which took place near Aldershot towards the end of the same year.

KING *v.* MACE.

"*Round* 1. The moment so fraught with interest and excitement to the partisans of the belligerents had now arrived; the busy and careful work of the seconds was at last completed to their entire satisfaction, and the men were delivered at the scratch. While their toilettes were being arranged, the 'making ready' had been eagerly watched by all with almost breathless silence. As Jem turned to face his opponent, he gave a momentary glance at the sky, whose dull, cheerless aspect was anything but calculated to enliven the combatants. Both advanced to the scratch with that firm, confident step which denotes the action of well-drilled practitioners. Perhaps the first thing that riveted the attention of the spectators, as the men stood front to front, was the striking difference in height that existed between them. It has been confidently stated Mace had never been in better condition; certainly as he stood thus confronting his antagonist there was nothing in his appearance that even the most fastidious could for a moment find fault with, and in all things he looked a far superior man to what he did at their former meeting. In weight Jem, when he last poised the beam, pulled down 11st. 4lb., and with inward confidence beaming in his every look, he stated that it was impossible for a man to feel better, and this assurance there can be no doubt had great weight with his admirers, many of whom from over-caution had waited for this 'opinion' from Mace himself before they ventured to 'put it on.' If condition of itself could alone endow a man with the requisite 'resin' to tune the first fiddle in such a grand pugilistic overture, Tom might well put the thing down as a 'certainty,' for it must be admitted that he was all the most critical could desire, and spoke of the result with a confidence devoid of anything in the shape of braggadocia. The moment the men had been 'set' by their seconds, there were perceptible that twitch and shrug of the shoulders which denote a disapproval of the morning air. Jem having put up the prop in proper order, drew from range, and of his position it may be said the skill of the master was at a glance displayed, for he was well covered at all points. Tom also stood remarkably well, and although by some good judges he is stated to be a little too fine about the loins, and by no means deep set enough in the jaw and neck, yet we think it was conceded by all impartial persons that he looked a most formidable opponent. Mace, as he manœuvred, looked at his man with a sharp penetrating glance, as though he was mentally summing up 'the King's affairs.' The result seemed satisfactory, for Jem gave one of his well-known jerks of his nob, as much as to say, 'Tom, I intend to give you another dressing.' King smiled at his man, as to intimate, if he really imagined he was capable of dressing him again he would oblige by being quick about it, as there needed something in the shape of excitement to warm up the system. After a little sparring Mace drew from range and dropped his mauleys, and then with his right rubbed his breast and arms. King imitated his action, as he felt numbed about the arms, and thought it necessary to do the burnishing to promote the circulation. Jem, with a cautious step, drew into range, and then by way of a feeler slightly let go the left, but Tom, who was decidedly quicker on his pins than we had found him in any of his preceding battles, got well away with the back step, thus showing that these efforts on the part of his opponent to draw out his guard were not likely to be successful. As Mace broke for the purpose of getting from distance, King dashed at him in a most impetuous manner, and missed administering a fine right-handed shot from the fore-arm. Mace, as Tom came on for the purpose of forcing the fighting, retreated, but just opposite the referee and umpire the men closed, when Jem, finding he was likely to get in an awkward position, ducked his head and went down, King looking at him. Both men were loudly cheered, and as there was just a shade of commotion among those who formed the uprights of the outer circle, Professor Duncan, attended by the 'faculty,' promptly administered a mild dose of his efficacious remedy for disorder—the 'syrup of whips'—and the cure was instantaneous.

2. At the call of 'Time,' both men, with the eagerness of swimmers for the first plunge, rushed simultaneously from the knees of their seconds, and threw up their hands at the scratch. After toeing the mark, each again drew back from range, and began rubbing himself, looking meanwhile at each other like two game-cocks. Mace then led with the left, but did not get it home, as King got well from range. Tom now dashed at his man, and delivered the left on the top of the head, and put in another from the fore-arm on the mouth, which had the effect of producing a slight show of the crimson. ('First blood,' as on the former occasion, for Tom.) Jem, after getting home slightly with the left and right on the face, closed with his man, when, finding he was likely to get into an awkward position, he slipped from him and got down, there being so far not much harm done on either side, King fighting with remarkable fairness; his opponent decidedly more crafty and shifty, though, as Jack Macdonald said, 'We'll give him all that in.'

3. Jem was the first from his corner, but no sooner did the busy seconds of King see that his

antagonist was on the move than they gave the office, and with that impetuosity of action so characteristic of him, he at once advanced to the scratch. After shifting, changing position, and taking fresh ground, King went dashing at his man for the purpose of forcing the fighting, and, getting partly over Jem's right cross-guard, planted the left on the right cheek, and with a wild, slinging round hit from the right also got home on the side of the knowledge-box. Mace, in the counter-hitting, administered one with his stinging left on the jaw, when, as Tom was not to be kept out, they closed. In the struggle for the fall King got his right arm round his man, and they went down near the referee in a curious awkward fall, Mace, who had his head bent down, hitting the top part of it against the ground. It was imagined by many at the moment that Jem might have received some severe harm, but they were soon convinced to the contrary, for when the men had become disentangled, and Jem, with his usual agility, had righted, he looked up with a broad grin, as much as to say, 'Don't be uneasy, I'm all right.' There was in the excitement again a slight manifestation of pressure in 'court,' the 'special jury' being the least bit inconvenienced, but Duncan, as head usher, brought up his efficient corps to point, and the weight of this legal element was on the instant sufficient to restore matters to their proper balance, and the business of this admirably-kept ring went on as smoothly as ever.

4. While the combatants were in their corners every movement of their seconds was watched with the utmost minuteness, and it was a treat to observe in what fine order they sent them to the mark. Tom was the first to present his towering height at the scratch, but was almost on the instant met by his opponent. Bos Tyler pointed at Mace, in a good-humoured manner, as much as to intimate Jem had had some of the burnishing powder. Mace feinted with the left, but finding he could not get in with artistic effect, he did not let it go freely from the shoulder. Tom, for the purpose of taking better range, followed up, and with the left got home on the right cheek, and also put in one from the right. As Mace broke to get away, Tom hit out with both mauleys, but did no execution, as Mace threw the left off well with the right guard. After slight sparring and manœuvring Tom led the left, but it was not sent sufficiently well in to be effective, nor did he meet with any better success in following up

with a wild hit from the right, for Jem drew well out of range. On again coming to distance, King worked with his right arm backwards and forwards, as though he intended to let it go, but did not. As Jem shifted, Tom followed, when Mace got home a fine left-handed lift on the jaw. The combatants in the most spirited manner fought across the ring, Mace administering some of the cayenne with both mauleys. In the close both struggled for the fall, when Tom got from his man and went to grass in his own corner.

5. Mace was the first to come from his corner, but he had not long to wait before Tom faced him. Both men were considerably pinked, and their physiognomies now possessed more touches of beauty than are to be found in their photographs in George Newbold's collection of celebrities. Jem, as he came from his corner, bent his head forward, as though he was mentally debating in what new manner he should try to get well at his man, who, by the rapid style in which he had been fighting, had given proof that he was a dangerous antagonist. King, the instant he had put up his hands, went dashing to force the fighting. With the left he administered a stinger on the right cheek, and followed up with a half-round hit from the right.

Mace, as his opponent rushed at him to close, drew out, but Tom, not to be denied, followed up, when, in a rally, Jem pegged away with both mauleys, left and right, with astonishing rapidity, doing a great deal of heavy execution. In the close they struggled for the fall, when Mace threw his man in clever style near the ropes. (The friends of Mace were in ecstasies, and long odds were offered on their pet.)

6. Tom in the first two or three rounds had unquestionably had a shade the best of it, from the style in which he had gone dashing at his man, and the quickness he had displayed. Mace did not exhibit that steadiness in his practice he afterwards did. Now, however, that Jem had got the true measure of his man there was a total change in his tactics, and the manner in which he now fought proved that he was in all respects superior to the 'big-'un' in science. Both, on presenting themselves at the mark, bore evidence of having been by no means idle, for Jem was swelled about the ivories in a very conspicuous manner, while King, from the appearance of his left peeper, gave unmistakable proof of having been warmed up; he was likewise slightly bleeding from the nose. Still there had been no serious damage done on the part

of either. After some little manœuvring, the combatants changing and shifting position, King dashed at his antagonist in his usual style, getting home left and right on the head. Mace met his man as he came with the rush on the milling suit, and, in one of the finest rallies that could be witnessed, the combatants fought right across the ring; there was something delightful to the admirers of boxing in Jem's style of fighting his man with both hands, left and right, at the nob. These blows were delivered with a rapidity that was quite electrifying, being sent ding-dong, straight home, so that Jem was all over his man in an instant, the blows making an impression as though Tom had been stamped with a couple of dies. Tom was by no means idle, but also pegged away at his man with the left on the head and the right on the body in merry fashion. In the close they got on the ropes, when Jem for the moment touched the top cord with his right hand, but Tom having shifted his position, the men struggled for the fall, when Tom, as a termination to this well-fought round, was under.

7. As the battle progressed, so did it increase in interest, for there was a marked speciality about the manner in which it was being fought that could not

possibly fail to enhance its importance among the admirers of bold and genuine boxing. There can be no disputing, both men had been from the commencement fighting remarkably well, and the battle, as will be seen, had already presented two striking and prominent features; for though until Jem had thoroughly got the measure of his man, King had in the opening bout been considered to have a slight lead, yet the style in which Mace was now performing was sufficient to convince all that there had not been the slightest mistake made in his merits as regards milling excellence. The combatants came simultaneously from their corners. Tom, as he stood at the scratch, opened his mouth and rubbed his hands, and then, on again putting himself into position, drew out and retreated to his own corner, Mace following. Both, as they again drew to range, steadied themselves, and in a fine counter with the left got well home, Jem doing execution on the snout, Tom on the top part of the cranium. Mace, on breaking, got to the ropes, when, as Tom came boring in to close, he slipped from the embrace of the young giant and got down.

8. From the manner in which the tints had been rubbed in, it was apparent the colours had been

well worked up, though this was much more conspicuous on Tom's dial than his opponent's, for King's left peeper had a small lump on the side of it, while the nose and mouth looked a good deal puffed. Tom, as usual taking the initiative, lunged out the left, but did no execution, as he was not well to distance. Mace, after King had opened with this wild hit, took up fresh position, and in doing so, as he was followed by his antagonist, he hit the back part of his head against the stake. As Tom pressed in, Jem pulled himself together, and after some fine left-handed counter-hitting, in which Mace delivered very heavily on the middle of the head, they closed and went down, Mace through the ropes. The battle had now lasted twenty-two minutes, and it had been nothing but downright hard fighting, and no mistake.

9. King made another dash at Jem, 'on hostile thoughts intent,' and got home apparently a hot-'un on the right eye, but there was no sign of injury, evidently owing to Jem's excellent condition. Jem instantly returned a severe prop on the dial with the left, and then countered a second effort on the part of King, who essayed his right. Tom, desperate, now dashed in with head-strong determination, and bored his man through the ropes, to the delight of

the Kingites, who, however, declined to take 6 to 4, freely offered by the backers of Mace.

10. Mace, the instant the signal was given, came forth with the utmost alacrity to renew the struggle. King, as an opening to the attack, lunged out the left, and administered a telling spank on Jem's right jaw; and then as Tom came dashing on, the men fought in a fine two-handed rally, right across the ring, when King got his man's nob for an instant in the right-arm lock, and pegged away in the fibbing beautifully. Jem, like a good tactician, extricated himself; and after some severe milling, in which Mace got in the most telling manner on his man's mouth, cheek, and nose—going, in fact, all over the dial with his clenched digits in a rapid and surprising manner—the men closed at the ropes right opposite the umpire and referee, when Jem got his man in position, and gave him a fair back-heel fall. Immense cheering for Mace.

11. King's left eye looked worse than ever, while his good-looking mug was knocked out of all symmetry. Nevertheless he was again first to begin the attack, and in leading got home the left on the right cheek, following it with one from the right on the side of the pimple. Jem, who timed his man beautifully, administered another

tremendous left-hander on the mazzard, when Tom's nob, from its effect, went waving back. On the instant, however, he pulled himself together and dashed in to renew the struggle, when Jem met him and delivered a tremendous left-hander on the nose, which produced a copious flow of blood. As Mace took fresh ground Tom again dashed in, and they fought a regular ding-dong slogging give-and-take to a close. Tom, with his usual style of bending his head slightly forward, went dashing at Jem, and got more than one straightening prop. They again fought in regular ding-dong to a close, when Tom, while receiving Jem's props on the dial, made use of the right once or twice in a very efficient manner on the body, upon which Mace got from his man and went down. The referee here called the attention of Tom's seconds to the fact that their man had struck Jem while he was down, which was true; but Mace was just on the go, and King could not help the hit, which was evidently unintentional, and no harm was done.

12. Another splendid rally in this round, Mace again in a telling manner doing execution with both mauleys, but evidently forced back by King's irresistible advance. The men, who had fought

right across the ring, closed in Mace's corner, when Jem got down, Tom falling on him. During this round the referee had several times to caution the seconds, who, in a most reprehensible manner, followed their principals so closely as frequently to be in the way of the combatants.

13. The men again went to work in a spirited and determined manner. Jem, with his left, got well home on the front of his man's dial, and jumped back; when Tom, with his right, administered some sounding spanks on the ribs. As Jem broke to get away, King followed him up, and Mace went down to end the round.

14. Mace commenced operations by getting well in range and delivering a pretty left-hander full on the nose, knocking Tom's head round as though it had been shaken off its connections; nevertheless Tom again tried to force the fighting, when, after some merry exchanges, they closed, and in the fall went down together in the centre of the ring. King's friends cheered him heartily, as he fully deserved.

15. Some sharp fighting, rather in favour of Mace, who, in the end, went down in the hitting, and King fell over him.

16. Tom dashed in viciously, and after a fine

exchange of compliments, in which each did execution, they closed, and Jem, who had had the best of the exchanges, fell under.

17. Tom again forced the fighting, but though he delivered with his left, he was a little too round with his right to be effective. Mace, after countering with his antagonist, and getting well home with the left in the middle of the head, and following up at half measure with the right, got cleverly away from his man. As Jem took fresh position, Tom followed him up, and the men in a rally fought to the ropes. In the close both got under the top rope and fell nearly out of the ring.

18. Such certainty was the battle looked upon by some of Jem's admirers, that Johnny Gideon here offered £30 to £5 on him, but there were no takers. Indeed, Tom's umpire, a good judge, said that, bar accident, Mace could not lose. After some more severe fighting, in which Mace again delivered in a telling manner on Tom's dial with both mauleys, Tom made a slip in getting from his man and fell on his knees. On the instant the game fellow recovered his perpendicular, and as Jem noticed this he beckoned him to renew the round. King was willing, but his well-skilled seconds, seeing the fast work he was doing, refused to allow him.

DRAW FOR THE CROSS COUNTER.

19. It now seemed 'all over but shouting' to the partisans of Mace, who called out any odds without response. As the men came up it was easy to see that Jem, thinking himself already victorious, was anxious to finish off the business, lest the appearance of the police, which had been rumoured, should rob him of his conquest at the last moment. He worked in with both hands in weaving style to get well to distance, and as he took up his position he got into a slight hollow on the ring. Jem, who had repeatedly tried to land a clipping cross-counter with his right, had just opened himself with the purpose of trying it on, when Tom, who stood firmly to his guns, met him with one of the most tremendous hits we ever saw. It was a cross-counter on the left cheek, with his right hand—a blow that seemed to go all over Jem's face with crushing effect. Jem, bleeding from the mouth and nose, reeled and staggered from the effect of this visitation, and then, to the consternation of friends, fell in the middle of the ring all of a heap. So sudden a change in the aspect of affairs had hardly ever been witnessed in the memory of the oldest ring-goer, and Jem's seconds were working with a zeal which told how serious was the position. Down came the odds.

'The Champion's licked,' said twenty voices in a stage whisper, and all eyes were strained in the direction of the busy group in Mace's corner.

20. King walked up to the scratch, watching the referee with ill-concealed anxiety to hear the call of 'Time.' When, however, that functionary had twice repeated his summons, Mace, who had by no means recovered from the settler he had received, came unsteadily from his corner. Tom walked up to him, and Mace tried a wild delivery with his left, Tom retorted with a hot blow on the nose, and Mace, in getting away, went down close to the referee's seat like a lump of lead. There was now the greatest commotion and excitement all round the ring. It was now as clearly King's victory as it had previously been Mace's. Brettle and Travers worked with a will, doing for their man everything possible, and he gallantly seconded their efforts, resolutely refusing to allow them to throw up the sponge.

21 and last. Before Mace left his corner Tom was waiting for his man, and no sooner did Mace come up than King went to him, and, with a slight push on the head, sent him down. Jem, who was weak and exhausted, and who had the right side of his phiz swelled in an extraordinary manner

from the effects of King's right-hander, was now clearly *hors de combat*, and his friends, seeing he had not the remotest chance of winning, threw up the sponge in spite of his protests. This token of defeat was hailed with loud shouts by Tom's friends, who were, of course, doubly delighted at the bravery and good fortune of their man, and they crowded enthusiastically round King to hail him as the last addition to the roll of brave men who have borne the proud title of Champion of England. The battle lasted exactly thirty-eight minutes."

It appears probable that Mace lost his chances through over-eagerness to knock his man out, and so terminate the fight in his own favour. Both men were clearly extremely exhausted, having honestly done their best in the twenty-one severe rounds, but to King was granted the advantage of having the best hit left in him at the finish, and he was able to make use of it. At the conclusion of the fight, strange though it may appear, Jem Mace was hardly what might be called severely punished—he was indeed far fresher than after his former fight in which he defeated King.

We now pass on to the consideration of a highly important question—that of natural aptitude. Art will do a great deal, incessant practice will do more, careful training will almost work miracles, but if nature has not given the initial impress of *suitability*, the highest prominence will never be attained.

A man intended by nature to lift heavy weights and go through slow strength feats will show it in his *form* and *movements:* you can measure his activity with the eye, and see that he is slow, and will never step into the first rank. The man himself may think differently, and painfully plod along with his boxing in the vain hope that from his great strength, and by dint of practice, he may some day become a shining light in the pugilistic world. He never will; but his effort is praiseworthy, and he will no doubt enormously improve, and be a far more formidable antagonist than he would be *without* his boxing knowledge.

These remarks are not intended to discourage but rather to warn people against expecting great returns in quarters where the raw material is not of the very first quality.

Take Jem Mace, for instance. His rounded limbs, in which no indication of rigid muscles is visible, his broad chest, square shoulders, powerful loins, and rather small calves, all point to speed and activity. Then take Sandow or Sampson or any of these "strength feats" men, and compare their limbs with those of the celebrated old fighter; you will notice the difference at once. Men with rigid muscles and large joints are usually slow, because it takes an appreciable time to unbend those muscles, and there is as much difference in their hitting powers and those of quick loose hitters as there is between the kicking powers of a cart-horse and a race-horse.

Again, it is rare to find a very large man who is "handy" and quick. Your giant, too, is often weak in some point—apt to get groggy on his pins, is often flabby and ill-set up, and his circulation, possibly because his heart has to pump the blood over such a large area, may be sluggish. Then, though reach and weight are present, the necessary speed is very often absent. And we thus find the best all-round men amongst the middle weights, *i.e.* 11st. 4lbs. and slightly under, for they have *enough* weight to make their blows effective, and are frequently as quick as the best light weights.

CHAPTER XVI.

INSTRUCTION AND TRAINING.

ANYTHING which makes a man really uncomfortable, and interferes ever so little with his appetite or his sleep, cannot be good for training; and a man who finds himself unable to go through any such course without inconvenience should leave training alone, and go in for an extra share of the particular sort of athletics he is preparing for.

There are, however, few men who are not the better for a judicious course of dieting; and as soon as they realize how important it is to modify certain of their habits or pleasures, it will not be such a very up-hill business.

Of course the first thing is to get the blood into a thoroughly healthy state, for when there is any congestion in any organ there is a weak point at once. Plenty of fresh air and exercise is therefore of the first importance. Then the different organs, *e.g.* kidneys, stomach, etc., should not be overtaxed by excess of drink or food, and the articles consumed should be *such as are most readily assimilated by the individual in training*. No one would suggest training a boat's crew on lobsters, for instance, in preference to beef-steaks; but, if one man in the crew could eat these crustaceans with impunity and benefit, and loathed beef, it would be far better to let him feed *in moderation* on his own chosen diet.

The same to some extent applies to smoking. A couple of pipes a day might be highly prejudicial to the training of some men, and be of the greatest service to others, and especially to those who have been used to a good deal of smoking.

Training is really very well understood in the present day, and it is also recognized, more completely than it was in years gone by, that in addition to attention to the idiosyncrasies of individuals, there is the consideration of the nature of the sport, or the *duration* of the muscular effort required.

The skin should always be kept in a healthy state of activity by exercise (at stated intervals), not often carried to the length of producing fatigue. The elimination of much dross in the system may be effected by means of Turkish baths, but remember that whilst in the bath you are not working and improving your muscles, you are simply sweating in a lazy manner; but if you are skipping, hitting the sack, or boxing, you are both sweating and improving your circulation and strength. Neither the bath nor the exercise should be *overdone* on any account.

After every spell of exercise a good rub down with a rough towel, and a change of garments is highly desirable; the former tends to close the pores of the skin, and to produce a healthy glow, and the latter prevents the chance of taking a chill.

Most people are the better for a cold bath in the morning, but if there is the slightest doubt about its agreeing or affecting the liver, or making the bather "froggy" or "clammy," it should at once be given up as harmful.

Perhaps the most cleanly and satisfactory bath of all is that which is taken as hot as possible, and whilst the skin is all aglow, even to redness, a thoroughly cold shower all over for about half a minute.

The older one gets the more difficult it is to

train with any sort of satisfaction to oneself or any one else. Up to thirty it is all right, between thirty and forty it is laborious and vexatious, but after forty it becomes heroic, so far as the vast majority of men are concerned. It is not difficult to get a youngster to give up any pet habit—such as eating pastry or smoking—for the short time he may take to get fit, but many an old fellow will be quite miserable if you altogether deprive him of his baccy and beer for the lengthened course to which he will probably have to submit.

In all cases of training, whether with the youthful or elderly, *do nothing abruptly*. Gradually slack off the indulgences and vices, so that their absence is hardly noticed. The older the man the slower the process.

The training for boxing is, as a rule, very similar to that required for rowing, the difference being that it is often necessary in boxing training to get a man's weight down below a certain standard to enable him to enter for some particular class, whilst in rowing it is always desirable to keep the weight up, and it is looked upon as a good sign if the avoirdupois increases as the time of the race draws nigh.

Needless to say, the exercise you get from

boxing itself should form the chief item in your course of training. Next in order of importance comes the knocking off of superfluous tissue by means of judicious dieting, and the third desideratum is a sufficiency of *open air* exercises, such as running, skipping, or hitting at the sack.

Two or three times a week only it will be well to go in for really fatiguing rehearsals of what you may expect on the day of the actual contest, and to do this it will be well to get two or three men to take you on, so that in each of your rounds you may have a fresh man to tackle. It will be well to go in for a couple, or even three bouts of three rounds each, in this way, since you may have to box in several heats on the day of the competition.

The question of how much fatiguing work should be done in the course of the week is one which must be left a great deal to the discretion of the trainer and to the man himself. Some men cannot stand much very heavy work, whilst others seem to improve with it. Generally speaking, it would be well to consider boxing for an hour or so a day, together with plenty of out-door work, as suggested above, sufficient to form an excellent framework for any kind of boxing preparation.

INSTRUCTION AND TRAINING. 313

Much depends upon the *kind* of contest and its probable duration.

Tom Sayers exhibited great staying powers, and some of his fights lasted a long time, but he was always a poor hand at *training*, properly or improperly so called in those days.

In fights of the old days the "rounds" were often extremely short—sometimes only half-a-minute—a man went down, obtained recuperation from mother earth, and then went on gaily again. In the present day, even in a three-round contest, with three and four minute rounds, the fighting, all to be shown in ten minutes, is generally very fast and furious, and a man should be in really good condition to do himself justice.

If weight has to be reduced, the use of a couple of sweaters during the skipping practice, or whilst running or hitting the sack, is to be placed far ahead of the Turkish bath.

The last fortnight of the training should be the hardest, but no *fatiguing* work should be done for the two days immediately preceding the contest. This may, of course, be varied to suit the individual; the reason for the advice is that all hard work is somewhat inimical to speed.

And now to a point which has hardly received

sufficient attention. The preparation for any kind of prolonged effort should include the use of only those accessories which tend to assist in the cultivation of what is really required. For example, heavy dumb-bells or clubs, though not detrimental for rowing training, would be quite out of place, and absolutely deleterious for boxing, in which only the lightest dumb-bells—say 3lbs. or even 2lbs.—and clubs should be used.

Skipping for twenty minutes at a time—three times a day—is excellent, and this, with a smart run, morning and evening, will keep the legs nimble and elastic; and hitting at the sack, say for ten minutes twice a day, will, in conjunction with the boxing, get the upper portion of the body used to the effort of long-continued punching.

The punching-sack should be stuffed tightly with flock, hay, or cloth, and should be about 3ft. long, and should be suspended from a beam in such a way that the upper portion is about on a level with the head of an ordinary man, and it is a good plan to chalk a line round the sack, to represent the belt, below which you must not hit. When punching the sack use boxing-gloves, and keep on hitting out rapidly with both hands. Five minutes of this will be found fatiguing, but if you can keep it up for ten minutes so much the better, and the effort is worth making.

Rowing is fine exercise, but being of the nature of weight-lifting is not to be commended as a preparation for fighting. A little light paddling would probably do no harm, and a spin in a sculling boat might do good, but anything like a severe strain in this direction would, in my opinion, be prejudicial.

In further reference to dieting, farinaceous foods have been rather tabooed as fattening and weight-producing; still, men have trained, and trained *well*, on a diet in which oatmeal porridge formed the chief ingredient.

Good beef, chopped up fine with bread-crumbs and salt, followed by a small portion of stewed prunes and well-cooked rice, would do well for the mid-day meal, which should be *the* meal of the day, and a glass or two of prime old ale goes well with this diet, and does the ordinary man no harm whatever, *i.e.* supposing him to be strong and healthy, and to be able to digest anything wholesome which is placed before him.

The circumstances of a man's deteriorating during training is one which should be at once gravely considered, and every effort should be made without any delay to discover the *cause*. Possibly the diet may not suit him, or the amount of exercise may be too much for him. Whatever it is, *some* changes must be made. The diminution of liquids may have been brought about too suddenly, or he may miss something he has been generally accustomed to. If he complains of lassitude towards evening, try slightly lessening the amount of exercise, and substitute a small bottle of champagne for his meals instead of beer on alternate days.

The following distribution of working, feeding, and sleeping during the twenty-four hours is suggested, as suitable to the ordinary young man:—

Rise at 6 a.m.; drink a small glass of pure spring water; put on flannels, and take a few short runs—a hundred yards, two or three times—and do a little skipping for say half-an-hour. Soon after 6.30 have a hot bath, followed by an icy-cold douche or shower, and a good rub down with rough towels. Dress and get ready for breakfast at seven. Do not make a *heavy* meal, and eat sparingly of those things only which you find you can easily digest. Fried sole or plaice, mutton-chops, poached eggs, a little porridge, dry toast, marmalade, and wholesome fruit in season should be a sufficiently extended *menu* from which to select your morning food. A cup of cocoa made with boiling milk, or a cup of weak tea should do for drink. Coffee is not recommended, as it is heating, and is rather too strong a stimulant.

Take it easy after breakfast, *i.e.* write your letters, smoke one pipe only, and do anything in the way of light business you may have to do. At ten o'clock go for a good walk in flannels, varying the walking with short spells of sprinting; return at eleven o'clock and practice sparring for an hour and a half, after which have a dry rub down with rough towels (no bath this time), and change into clean dry things, and be ready at 1 p.m. to tackle the chief meal of the day. Though it is the fashion to rather decry soups, it would appear advisable, as a means of making a pleasant change, to give a small plate of the most nourishing soup on alternate days; wholesome fish, such as cod, turbot, sole, plaice, being provided on the other days. Oysters, when in season, may be also recommended. Beef and mutton suit most men, but these should be varied by chickens and game. All rich curries or made dishes of all kinds should be studiously avoided, as well as hot sauces and pickles. Good stewed fruit, with any sort of well-boiled "fixing" in the shape of rice, corn-flour, sago, or macaroni, may safely be recommended when the pudding stage is reached. Do not eat much *uncooked* fruit, and avoid all nuts. Old ale or champagne *in great moderation* should accompany this meal.

After dinner allow a clear hour to elapse before you think of doing any exercises, and then at 3 or 3.30 p.m. get into your flannels and proceed with the serious work of the day—skipping, Indian clubs, light dumb-bells, punching the sack, together with one bout of three rounds as prescribed by the rules under which you are to compete. This bout should be the hardest of the day, and after it is over you may swing the light clubs for twenty minutes, and then have a good rub down and get into your dry clothes. This will bring you to 6.30 or 7 p.m., when you will be quite ready for the final light repast of the day, and this should consist of the lightest and most digestible food you can get hold of. Cold minced chicken, minced beef with bread and salt, or a good plate of thoroughly well-boiled mutton-broth, may be recommended with safety; and after the meal, if no other drinks but water have been taken, a glass of fine old port will do no harm.

INSTRUCTION AND TRAINING. 319

At 9.30 take a short turn in the open air, and get to bed at ten o'clock, for the eight hours' sleep which will carry you on to six o'clock the following morning.

The above suggestions will only be of use to those who can give so much time in the day to their preparation; the great majority of men are employed in offices, or at some other work during all the best hours of the day, and the sedentary employment forced upon them is not good for training, so that, whenever possible, a fortnight's holiday should be secured just before the competition comes off.

It suits many men remarkably well to get a week at the sea-side just before the contest, and remember that in all cases no *hard* work should be done for the last day or two.

You want a combination of wind and strength, so that care must be taken not to over-train, and as regards getting rid of fat and adipose tissue, if it is found impossible to do this without injuring the staying powers, it will be safer to leave it alone and send the man up for the higher class: *i.e.* if you find that your somewhat aged "13-stunner" cannot get down to 11st. 4lbs. without becoming stale and seedy, or even showing a slight falling off in his energy of attack, give up all ideas of sending him in for the middles, and let him keep on training steadily, and without much effort to reduce his weight, for the heavies. I should say it is never a good plan to "train fine" for boxing; there always seems a lack of punching power in the man who is so beautifully trained that you can see his backbone through his stomach.

Men grow stouter, as a rule, with advancing years, and this is partly caused by their having too much money, and being able to drive in cabs and carriages where they formerly walked, and partly from leaving off the athletic and healthy occupations of their earlier youth.

Except in very rare instances it takes a long time to bring a man of forty or upwards into anything approaching the old form of fifteen years previous. The process must be very gradual; the luxuries have to be knocked off with a sparing hand, and not all at once, otherwise he gets miserable, and the cheerfulness which goes hand-in-hand with good digestive powers, deserts him at the very time when it is most needed. Everything, however, depends upon the individual: some active men of forty will train quicker than phlegmatic "stodgy" young fellows of twenty-five, but the rule is that the "old 'un" wants a lot of care because his habits are so formed. You *bend* the youth, but you may *break* the old gent altogether if too rough with him!

To some men a large share of sleep is a necessity, and the eight hours above suggested may seem to them quite a moderate allowance. Others would be quite happy and satisfied with six hours; we may safely take it that the allowance should vary between six and eight, and that as a rule we require less as we get older.

If the work is severe, and the evening finds a man jaded, it is often a sound policy to insist on his lying down for an hour in the middle of the day. This siesta often has a wonderfully reviving effect, and the afternoon's serious and hard sparring is looked forward to with gusto instead of being dreaded as a bore and a nuisance. Then again, some people absolutely hate getting up early in the morning; it is *better* to get up early for the sake of the morning air and freshness, but if it is positively injurious it must be discontinued.

When taking outdoor exercise let the expirations and inspirations be as complete and full as possible. All the vitiated air is thus expelled, and the lungs are able to receive the next breath.

If business avocations keep you from ten to four at what are called sedentary pursuits, endeavour to get a high desk, so as to relieve the monotony of constantly sitting at your work. Of course in this case your training must suffer, for it will be carried on under difficulties. For instance, the city clerk has not time to make his chief meal in the middle of the day, he may but snatch half-an-hour or so for a snack about one o'clock, and this will necessitate a late dinner of far more solid proportions than that indicated above. He should also make a more substantial matutinal feed, and he will have to retire to rest later. If he dines at, say, eight o'clock, he cannot think of going to bed till 11 or 11.30, as it would not be wise, for the sake of digestion, to do so.

To partially meet the difficulty a little extra skipping or punching the sack may be put in before breakfast, and ten minutes' Indian clubs before getting into bed. The serious work must be all squeezed into the two hours between five and seven in the afternoon.

A little mild physic is usually beneficial at some period of the training, but any attempt to reduce weight by repeated physicking is to be deprecated most emphatically. Rhubarb pill and citrate of magnesia, or Eno's fruit salt will do very well, but they should not be resorted to when all the functions of nature are being carried on with perfect regularity and satisfaction. "Take care of the pence, and the pounds will look after themselves." Take plenty of exercise and sufficiency of good food, drink, and sleep, and all other matters will require but little attention.

There are many good instructors to be found in London, and my advice to any beginner is that he should as soon as possible put himself in the hands of a really first-rate "professor" of the Noble Art, so that he can practically work out what he has been reading about in books. The various points will one by one be demonstrated beyond a doubt, and he will find out the correctness of his first principles, and really understand the whys and the wherefores. At Cambridge, my old instructor, George N. Jackson, is a good man to teach, and there are numbers of competent professionals in London, including Ned Donnelly, Bat Mullins, and George Roberts.

CHAPTER XVII.

CATCHES, FALLS, AND IN-FIGHTING.

WHEN two boxers or fighters get to close quarters, and the "clinching" game comes into play, there is apt to be a good deal of excitement resulting in wild struggling and straining for the throw, and the whole business looks ragged and unbusiness-like. It is not fighting proper, neither can it be called wrestling. A hybrid scramble in which the good points of both arts are all but indistinguishable.

When beginning to learn, it is not advisable to go in for close quarters business at all, but to keep entirely to leg work and long leads; but when the straight left has been to some extent mastered, and the *meanings* of the various positions and movements fairly well grasped, it will then be highly beneficial to practise in-fighting with all sorts of wild and rough fighters, as the more varied

DUCK TO LEFT WITH RIGHT-HAND HIT AT MARK—FOR MAN STANDING RIGHT FOOT FOREMOST.

your experience in this direction the more capable will you be of ultimately tackling with success any chance customer you may come across.

It is truly amazing what strange and altogether unexpected complications arise out of these clinches —your "natural fighter" as often as not does the last thing you would expect, and you may find yourself twisted into all sorts of contortions should you have failed to keep the adversary at a distance.

Putting aside the kicks of the "hobnailed rough," there are quite a sufficient number of other attacks to demonstrate the importance of constantly practising at close quarters—the greater the variety the greater the scope for the exercise and display of science.

When you get to close quarters, possibly in following up a body-blow or an upper cut, endeavour to take hits on the upper portion of your head, and use your own contracted-arm hits with a good swing of the shoulders and body; with the elbows bent till arm and fore-arm are at right angles, most effective hits can be given. The shoulder-joints will have to move a little, but if the arm, fore-arm, and shoulder are kept nearly solid, the power of the loins, back, and the weight of the body too, can be brought into play with excellent effect.

Be very careful, when in-fighting, not to let the hands get too low, and don't give a chance away or allow a semblance of doubt to creep in by *even touching the other man anywhere below the belt.*

Among the chief falls which result from in-fighting may be reckoned the "back-heel," the "back-fall," the "cross-buttock" and the "flying-buttock." These may be briefly described as follows—

In the true "back-heel" you strike the back portion of your opponent's left leg below the knee with your left heel, which you draw smartly back, at the same time pushing or hitting his head back with your arm or hand (*see* p. 114); if this is done quickly enough he will fall over backwards. The mere fact of your left leg acting as a stop to his saving himself by retreating *his* left leg is sufficient to give the fall without any striking of his leg with your heel. He cannot, if you are quick enough, well save himself with his right leg, and since you, as it were, hold his left leg, over he must go.

When the back-heel is tried upon yourself, your best defence is to rapidly throw the right leg back—a couple of feet or so—and this will give the necessary stability, and probably prevent the throw.

The "back-fall" is used as a reply to the "head-in-chancery trick," and may be effected with the *left* or *right* hand, according as your opponent has seized you with his *right* or *left* arm respectively. If he has your head under his right arm, you instantly bring your left hand round behind his back, so as to be able to get your hand over his face, or under his chin. You then press back his head, at the same time getting your left leg well behind his right, so that he may trip and fall over it backwards. (See p. 113.) In the other case, where he has your head under his *left* arm, you carry out exactly corresponding movements, only with your *right* arm, hand, and leg.

The back-fall is often a capital one when done quickly and neatly, but remember that in all cases of head-in-chancery there is the danger of the adversary's *retaining his hold in the fall*, and then your neck may suffer severely.

Again, if you think you can prevent the throw, it is often a good plan, the moment he gets his grip round your neck, to commence using both your short-arm hits alternately on his mark and kidneys—putting them in as hard and as rapidly as possible; by this means you have *two* punches for every one of his, and moreover your face is partly protected by the arm which you are using on his mark.

The "cross-buttock" arises when your head is in chancery, and the adversary, instead of punching you with his free hand, swings his hips round under you, drags you across them, and swinging his shoulders round in the same direction pitches you all of a heap in front of him. Here, as in the former cases, the fall may be a very serious one if he retains your head in chancery *during the fall*, and then falls upon you.

The cross-buttock may be either with the right or left arm; if with the former the cross-buttocker swings to the *right*, if with the left he swings to the left.

The "flying-buttock" is an extension of the foregoing, the difference being that the cross-buttocker gets you more completely over his loins and higher up, and swings you clean over his shoulder, and possibly you reach the ground head first.

The best general stop for the cross-buttock or flying-buttock is the back-fall described above, but you may also endeavour, should the above fail, to

THE UPPER-CUT.

CATCHES, FALLS, AND IN-FIGHTING. 329

swing your own body in the same direction as that in which he is swinging in order to get as much as possible in front of him, and thus avoid being dragged across his loins. Thus, if he has your head in chancery under his right arm, you will immediately, after swinging as above indicated, get your right hand well across his face (*see* p. 115), and force his head back to the utmost.

Occasionally after a spell of in-fighting, *but not in actually breaking away after a close or clinch*, you may administer an excellent upper cut, though this is a hit, as remarked elsewhere, which fails more often than it succeeds.

If you are quick enough, you may avoid the head-in-chancery business altogether by shooting the arm which is nearest the assailant's body sharply forward and upwards: by this means you get your shoulder in under his arm as well as your head and neck, and he cannot get a grip, and you can readily escape. My advice is *not* to try to get an assailant's head in chancery—it is not a very paying game as a rule, though you may sometimes take advantage of a lighter man in this way. If you should ever do this, remember that time is important, and hit him as often as you can with true contracted-arm hits, or short upper cuts, and then drop him. If he falls, well and good; if he continues to stand, instantly knock him down before he has time to recover his senses.

In the majority of the old fights there was a great deal of hugging, scragging, and clinching, and in the celebrated contest between King and Heenan in December 1863, this kind of thing was most marked. The betting was about 6 or 7 to 4 in favour of the Benicia Boy, and had it not been for King's excellent condition, and the fact that he possessed a straighter left and more science, the smaller man (King) could never have won as he did after a rough and tumble of thirty-five minutes' duration. In each of the first seven rounds King was scragged and heavily thrown.

In round 2 "Heenan made a dash at him, and showing great superiority in strength, after a few seconds of squeezing, threw him heavily, a very dangerous fall, coming with all his weight upon him." In the following round, the third, Heenan grappled him, and "again brought him down with shattering force across the lower rope, which was pressed to the ground." Heenan's mode of fighting was not approved of by the onlookers, but he was considered to be getting the best of the fight, as King could not resist his clinches. In this and in the following rounds it was remarked that Heenan's style of fighting was extremely bad, and that his hugging and squeezing were more perceptible than when he had fought Tom Sayers.

In round 5 King's straight-hitting powers stood him in good stead, and to some extent the Yankee was steadied and held in check, but he still managed his favourite clinch, and threw King heavily, though in doing so he pitched on his own head.

In round 6 Heenan again got his grip and threw King a regular burster, and at the end of round 7 Heenan closed in the hitting, hugged his man viciously, and then threw him one of the heaviest cross-buttocks seen for many a day. It was a crusher, and King lay quite still till his seconds picked him up and put him in his corner.

In round 8 King managed, much to the delight of his supporters, to pull off a really good "back-fall," thus frustrating Heenan's cross-buttock. After this the luck seemed to go with King for a few rounds, but when the fourteenth was reached, he was again thrown by one of the most tremendous cross-buttocks—probably the "flying-buttock"—ever seen. He was so completely shaken and stunned by this severe fall that it required all the cleverness of his seconds to bring him up to time. After this Heenan's eyes became so puffed up that it was evident he would soon be quite unable to see; still in the seventeenth round he managed to clutch his man desperately, and, with a last effort, threw him one of the hardest falls in the fight.

From this, on to the end of the fight, King had matters pretty well in hand, for he kept planting his straight hits on the rapidly closing optics of his antagonist, and in the twentieth round back-heeled him handsomely. After this Heenan became so groggy that he could only stagger on to meet his punishment just when and where King chose to administer it, and his backers threw up the sponge in the twenty-fourth round, when it was quite clear that no object was to be gained by putting up their man like a dummy to be hit at.

On this occasion Heenan proved conclusively, —so say those competent judges who witnessed the fight,—that he was not really even a second-rate boxer, for his continued and repeated attempts at strangulation and general roughing were opposed to all the correct ideas of fighting as it should be practised in the ring. Yet, notwithstanding the disparity in size and weight, Tom King's superior science told in the long run.

IN-FIGHTING.

A critic observed—"It was not the fault of Tom King that the fight was so bad. His form and style were far the better of the two, for he did not trust to mere wrestling and hauling his man about, and would have made a better show of tactics with a better man." King was not much marked, but Heenan was greatly disfigured, and almost blind at the conclusion of the contest.

"Altogether," continues the critic, "while an honest and game fight, it was an unsatisfactory one; the sole point settled being the entire absence on the part of Heenan, of those scientific attainments and steady attributes indispensable to the successful practitioner in the Prize Ring. The immense stake, £2000, so glaringly disproportionate to the merits of the battle, was duly paid over to King."

The above quotations, from an authentic account of this celebrated fight, appear to be particularly appropriate whilst on the subject of in-fighting.

We will now hark back to the days of Thomas Cribb, one of the greatest English Champions who flourished between 1805 and 1820, and describe two fights which took place between him and a powerful American black of African descent, Tom Molineaux. On their appearance on December

28, 1810, the men are thus described. Cribb, who stood 5ft. 10½in., weighed 14st. 3lbs.; while Molineaux, who was 5ft. 8¼in., was only a pound lighter, and consequently looked far more muscular. His arms were of wondrous length (like so many of his race) and roundness of form. The fight is thus described in *Pugilistica*—

CRIBB *v*. MOLINEAUX.

"*Round* 1. The combatants shook hands, retired two steps, put themselves in attitude, eyeing each other with the most penetrating looks, and each highly attentive to his guard. For a moment a solemn pause ensued. A little sparring, and Molineaux put in the first hit by a right-handed body-blow on the left side of his opponent. Cribb smartly returned right and left on the head, and one for luck on the body. Molineaux closed, and Cribb threw him. Thus the round ended without bloodshed.

2. Both set to with great eagerness, apparently fully determined on a manly stand-up fight, seeming to exclude sparring and shifting altogether. A furious rally, heavy blows exchanged. Cribb's did most execution, being thrown in straight

forward, while Molineaux struck hand over head with most astonishing power, but little judgment, and Cribb either parried or spoilt the effort, by planting the first hit. Cribb, although he showed first blood by a cut on the lip, evidently had the best of the round.

3. Molineaux faced his antagonist with great courage. Cribb met him with equal resolution, and after a little sparring brought his left fist in contact with his antagonist's head at arm's-length with such tremendous force, that he laid him to measure his full length on the earth. (4 to 1 on Cribb.)

4. Molineaux immediately jumped on his legs, and commenced a desperate rally, in which Cribb again brought him down.

5. An excellent round, good straightforward fighting, and both rallied in great style. Molineaux tried to bore down his opponent by main strength; Cribb determined to prevent him, if possible, by repeating some desperate blows on the head. They closed, and Molineaux fibbed very dexterously in Dutch Sam's style, but at length fell.

6. Molineaux commenced furiously. Cribb slipped, but partially recovered, and by a blow brought down Molineaux.

7. Molineaux rushed in as before, and Cribb put in a violent blow on the forehead, by which he picked up a handsome 'rainbow.' His countenance was, however, not the more clouded, and he was first to the time.

8. Both combatants by this time had been taught discrimination, and had discovered each other's physical powers. Cribb found out that his notion of beating Molineaux off-hand was truly fallacious, as he really was an ugly customer, and he also became sensible that if Molineaux could so reduce him as to make his sledge-hammer hits tell, he should not willingly lay his head for the anvil. He therefore now brought forward his science, and began to adopt his usual famous retreating system. The men rallied desperately; success was alternate. At length Molineaux fell; but Cribb, from his violent exertion, appeared weaker than his opponent.

9. Gallantly contested. Cribb made play, Molineaux followed courageously, giving no quarter, put in a severe hit, and Cribb fell, evidently much exhausted. The knowing ones looked queer; Cribb had been fighting too fast.

10. The conceit by this time was tolerably well taken out of both combatants; their heads and faces were hideously disfigured. Molineaux again dis-

CATCHES, FALLS, AND IN-FIGHTING.

played superiority of strength. For full two minutes hits were exchanged, greatly to the disadvantage of Cribb; he, however, at length brought down his opponent.

11. Courageously contested. Molineaux brought Cribb down.

12. Cribb put in a severe hit in the body. Molineaux returned on the head and fell.

17. Cribb still continued his shy plan, and Molineaux evidently had the advantage.

23. In this round Cribb, perceiving Molineaux falling off, made play and brought him down, the first time for several rounds.

24—28. Bets considerably reduced. They had been 4 to 1 on Molineaux, but were now even.

29. Molineaux ineffectually endeavoured to get Cribb's head under his left arm, and also to throw him, but failed in both. The men rallied, and Cribb, who now appeared to possess more confidence than he had for some rounds, knocked his opponent down.

30. Cribb now again got the lead, and stuck up to his opponent until he fairly rallied him down.

31. A short rally. Molineaux threw Cribb, but in the struggle fell over him, and pitched upon his head, which so severely affected him that he could

hardly stand. Richmond, however, prompted him to go on, in hopes of Cribb being exhausted.

33. Molineaux fell by an effort to keep his legs. This by Cribb's party was called falling without a blow, and a squabble would have ensued, had not Molineaux exclaimed, 'I can fight no more.'

Cribb was greatly elated at such a sound, but was too weak to throw his usual somersault. The contest lasted fifty-five minutes."

After this fight, in which both men were completely played out, and fought, so to speak, to a standstill, Molineaux, game fellow that he was, sent a challenge to Cribb, and a second encounter was arranged, and took place in September 1811, about nine months after the first fight. It was said at the time that Molineaux was rather given away, and that his training was not properly attended to, also that the remarks about him at the ring-side as a "man of colour," and the great preponderance of shouts in favour of his antagonist irritated and possibly cowed him. The stage on which these two giants fought was 25ft. square, and it seems probable that the hit on the mark in the sixth round practically decided the fight, which is now given *in extenso* :—

"*Round* 1. Sparring for about a minute, when

Cribb made play right and left. The right-handed blow told slightly in the body of Molineaux, who returned slightly on the head; a rally now ensued, they exchanged their blows, when Molineaux fell from a dexterous hit in the throat; the blows, however, throughout this round were not at a distance to do very great execution. Betting unaltered.

2. Cribb showed first blood at the mouth at setting-to. A dreadful rally commenced. Cribb put in a good body-hit with the right hand, which Molineaux returned on the head with the left flush; both combatants now fought at half-arm, and exchanged some half-dozen hits with great force. They then closed, and after a severe trial of strength Molineaux threw his opponent. Odds 6 to 4 on Cribb.

3. In the last rally Cribb's right eye was nearly closed, and now another equally sanguinary followed. After sparring for wind, in which essential Molineaux was evidently deficient, Cribb put in a dreadful 'doubler' on the body of his opponent, who, although hit away, kept his legs, and renewed the rally with such ferocity, that the backers of the odds looked blue. The rally lasted a minute and a half, when the combatants closed, and Molineaux

again threw Cribb with astonishing force. Odds fell, but Cribb's tried game still kept him the favourite.

4. In the rally Cribb had hit right and left at the body and head, but Molineaux fought at the head only. He was so successful with the left hand, that he planted many flush hits. Both Cribb's eyes were now damaged, his face dreadfully disfigured, and he bled profusely. Molineaux was evidently in great distress, his chest and sides heaving fearfully. Cribb smiled at such a favourable omen, and renewed the rally with a heroism, perhaps, never excelled, and, in point of judgment, most adroitly timed. Hits in abundance were exchanged, Cribb still fighting at the 'mark,' and Molineaux at the head; at length Cribb fell, evincing great exhaustion. Odds, however, were now 7 to 4 in his favour.

5. Molineaux accepted the rally, and the execution on both sides was truly terrific. Molineaux had the best of the exchanges, and Cribb fell from a blow, and in falling received another. This excited some murmurs and applause from the partisans of the contending heroes, and on reference to the umpires was decided 'fair,' Cribb's hands being at liberty, and not having yet touched the floor.

6. Molineaux, distressed for wind and exhausted, lunged right and left. Cribb avoided his blows, and then put in a good hit with his right, which Molineaux stopped exceedingly well. Cribb now got in a destructive blow at his 'mark,' which doubled up Molineaux; he got away pitifully cut up: he, however, returned to begin a rally, seemingly anxious to go in, but still sensible of the ugly consequences. He appeared almost frantic, and no dancing-master could have performed a pirouette more gratifying to Cribb's friends. Molineaux hit short, capered about, and was quite abroad. Cribb followed him round the ring, and after some astonishing execution, floored him by a tremendous hit at full arm's length. The odds rose 5 to 1.

7. Molineaux seemed lost in rage. He ran in, and undoubtedly did some execution; but Cribb put in several straight hits about the throat, stepping back after each. Molineaux bored in till he fell.

8. Molineaux again rallied, seemingly as a forlorn hope, but his distance was ill-judged. Cribb once and again nobbed him, and getting his head (his own trick by the bye) under his left arm, fibbed him until he fell.

9. Lombard Street to a China orange. Molineaux

was dead beat, and only stood up to encounter Cribb's ponderous blows. He ran in, Cribb met him with his left hand; the blow was tremendous, being doubled in force by the black's impetuous rush; Molineaux's jaw was fractured, and he fell like a log. He did not come up to time within the half-minute, but Cribb, wishing to show his superiority, gave away this chance, dancing a hornpipe about the stage, until—

10. With great difficulty Molineaux got off his second's knee, only for fresh punishment. His rush was desperate, but equally unsuccessful, and he fell evidently from distress.

11. Here ended the contest. Cribb gave away another chance in the time. Molineaux's senses, however, were absolutely hit out of him; he was perfectly unable to stand, and a Scotch reel by Gully and Cribb announced the victory, while the very welkin echoed with applause."

CHAPTER XVIII.

BAD EXAMPLES.

ANY two people who are constantly together are apt to fall into one another's ways, and copy peculiarities whether desirable or the reverse. This is very much the case in boxing, where you have a man constantly before you. It should, therefore, be your aim, first, to spar with good exponents of the art, or, second, if you cannot manage this, glean all the good you can by noticing the faults and correcting any tendency to them in your own style.

Some men have a particularly irritating and "jumpy" style; it is not that they know so very much, but they think that you may be taken in by it, and give them credit for what they don't deserve. Almost without knowing it you may find yourself engaging in the same unnecessary and unmeaning antics.

If you feel certain that your principles are

correct, never mind the other man, but go on steadily, and though you should constantly *vary* your tactics and plans to get at him, don't forsake the substance for the shadow by substituting a showy style for your own solid, good form.

One bad fault is that of "showing" the right in a sort of imaginary feint; the right should be held easily over the mark, and be ready at any moment to be brought into play.

Some men get into the way of sticking their tongues out; this is very easily copied. Keep the mouth firmly but not tightly closed, and if extra breath is needed, part the lips and inhale through the teeth. Only open your mouth wide when resting between rounds.

The gloves should be as small as possible, and well padded over the hitting knuckles, but never think of using them as guards. Your arms and hands are the only guards you should know anything about, and you have always to *box* as you would really *fight*.

The habit of turning round and slinking out of reach with the back turned to the opponent is a particularly bad habit; a retreat of this kind must be made sideways with an eye on the opponent.

Some boxers very readily acquire the habit of looking down at their adversary's feet in the hope

BAD EXAMPLES. 345

that he will be deceived by the ruse; never copy this, it is quite wrong, and leads to nothing, except with tyros.

Generally, do not copy any position or action which you cannot conscientiously pronounce "satisfactory" in your own mind. The reason why a book study of boxing principles is so beneficial is that it makes you *think* out the various intricate positions into which you may find yourself drawn or forced, and depend upon it that if the brain leads well, the hands and legs will be found ready and willing to carry out instructions. You may read of some particular attack or defence; think it over at night, and perhaps dream of it, and it is highly probable that this deep thought and consideration of possibly only one situation may be the means of giving you the necessary ideas which you may carry into effect on the next occasion the knowledge has to be put to practical use.

All your first ideas should be got from the best masters. Copy the style of Jem Mace, Nat Langham, Peter Jackson, Frank Slavin, or Robert Fitzsimmons, and *get to work with the best teachers you can;* at the same time *study* the subject from the best hand-books procurable, and never omit to ask the *reason why*.

CHAPTER XIX.

LA SAVATE.

AS a work on self-defence would hardly be complete without some reference to the kicking game, as practised in conjunction with *le boxe* in France, I have thought it well to introduce the following few remarks upon the subject.

In the *savate* you have, as it were, four weapons of attack, your two hands and two feet; there is no portion of the anatomy barred, and you are liable to be kicked anywhere from the crown of the head to the soles of the feet. The method has been described as fighting with four fists, and it is probable that situations may occur in which it may be useful, but a vast amount of nonsense has been talked about it, and its advantages have, in my opinion, been greatly overrated.

It is, for instance, contended that a good *savateur*

is more than a match for any four ordinary men, and I have seen an illustration representing an energetic individual who has been attacked by four men, two of whom he has placed *hors de combat* on the pavement; his left fist is planted in the

Fig. 8. Coup de Savate: First Kick.

middle of the face of his third assailant, whilst his left foot has *simultaneously* caught the remaining miscreant well on the point of the jaw. The gentleman thus depicted might truly say that his hands and feet were more than full: it reminds one of the Irishman writing home to his people

348 BOXING.

from the seat of war—"We are having glorious times; I am writing with a sword in one hand and a pistol in the other!"

Probably the chief drawback to the *savate* is the want of stability of position which is being constantly produced by this terpsichorean lifting of

Fig. 9. Parry for First Kick.

either leg. A man is constructed to stand on both feet, and in that position is most secure and *readiest to get about with rapidity:* directly you place him on one leg you restrict him to hopping, weaken his base, and so render him liable to be toppled over with great ease.

Then there is the difficulty of a satisfactory return from the complicated swings and twists of the legs to a decent position of defence—a serious matter when opposed to anything like first-class boxing.

The *coup de pied* may, if successful, do a great deal of damage; so may the "hook hit," so may many other forms of attack, but I feel bound to stoutly maintain the principle, that whenever aggressive measures lead to positions of great danger they should be avoided, and sounder, if less showy, tactics adopted. A prudent general does not venture into a hostile country without making sure of his retreat in the event of possible reverses. If you are *constantly* in a position—as you are when in any of the more favourite *savate* attitudes —from which recovery is difficult and slow, and in which, should the attack have proved a failure, you are dangerously exposed to the effects of rapid counter-attacks on the part of the adversary, you are, on all such occasions, seriously jeopardizing your chances of ultimate success.

You are, as it were, constantly risking too much, perhaps *your all*, on a single chance; and this game cannot surely be considered sound. Even if you were *completely* successful only once in five attempts you would not, in my opinion, be justified in running the risk, as the complications and disasters of the remaining four efforts would more than balance such success.

I here give a few outlines of some of the more favourite positions of attack and defence, and you

Fig. 10. Kick at the Mark.

will readily observe how unstable is the attitude in all of them.

Do not imagine that I am unduly running down the merits of the *savate*, such as they are, or that I am contending that the method has *no* advantages. To be able to deliver a really good *coup de pied* when attacked by roughs might on occasions turn out highly serviceable, but *in general*, and especially when opposed to British boxing of the first quality, I should not feel disposed to recommend it.

There are of course a number of kicks, all of which have different names; here we shall only mention a few of the principal ones. In the *coup*

Fig. 11. High Body-kick.

de savate the toe hits the opponent, in the *coup de flanc*, or side kick, the heel is brought to bear on him, and this is probably the severest kick of the two. Then there is the *chassé croisé* or cross-kick, and the *coup de pied tournant*, which is said to be both effective and dangerous when it "comes off."

Again, the *savateur* has a habit of kicking out

with one foot, simultaneously dropping on both hands, and swinging away out of reach in a truly acrobatic manner.

Of course if you stand up to a *savateur* and expect to be able to take him as you would spar

Fig. 12. Coup de Pied Tournant : First Position.

with an ordinary boxer, you will soon find your mistake ; one can readily imagine it to be a game which, when once sprung *unexpectedly* on even the best of boxers, might carry consternation into the camp! But, recognizing the dangers, and knowing what to expect, you will have to be on your guard, and ready for the slightest preliminary movements.

The first kick, for instance—the *coup de savate* (*see* p. 347)—is aimed at the lower portion of your left, or advanced leg, and the idea is to kick this leg from under you and so give you a fall to the left. This is why *savateurs* always have their

Fig. 13. Coup de Pied Tournant: Second Position.

entire weight on their hindermost leg, using the advanced limb much as a fencer uses a foil; the weight not being on this leg, a fall will not result when it is kicked away.

When standing in the ordinary boxing attitude as recommended in these pages, and in other hand-books on the subject, *i.e.* with the weight evenly balanced on both feet, the best defence to this low kick would probably be to withdraw the left leg altogether to the rear, and come into the position of a man standing right foot first, and then step rapidly in with right-hand hit at head or mark.

Fig. 14. Coup de Pied Tournant: Third Position.

For the higher kicks one should watch every opportunity of catching hold of the adversary's foot with both hands so as to give him a nasty fall.

By all means practise with *savateurs* if you get a chance. As far as I know, the comparative merits of the English boxing and the French combination of feet and fists have never been fairly and satisfactorily decided, but I have my own opinion as to the result of such a trial could it be made.

It would be interesting to get up an Assault at Arms at which the chief events might be a series of contests between, say, three picked *savateurs*

Fig. 15. One of the Stops.

and three picked English boxers, each individual on either side meeting, in turn, each one on the other side. There would, no doubt, be difficulties in arranging the *conditions*, and as regards judging, there might be a risk of ill-feeling springing up, partly on account of the different nationalities, and partly through the said conditions not satisfying the combatants on *both* sides.

CHAPTER XX.

DEFINITIONS AND RULES.

THE definition of an Amateur as generally accepted is—
"One who has never competed with or against a Professional for any prize, and who has never taught, pursued, or assisted in the practice of athletic exercises as a means of obtaining a livelihood."

Then there is the following rather more extended definition of a Gentleman Amateur—

"Any gentleman who has never competed in an open competition, or for public money, or for admission money, or with professionals for a prize, public money, or admission money, and who has never at any period of his life taught, pursued, or assisted in the pursuit of athletic exercises as a means of livelihood."

The Amateur Boxing Association, which has

DEFINITIONS AND RULES. 357

been in existence since 1884 or 1885, goes one better than these, and gives the following—

"An Amateur is one who has never competed for a money prize or staked bet, or with or against a Professional for any prize, except with the express sanction of the Amateur Boxing Association, and who has never taught, pursued, or assisted in the practice of athletic exercises as a means of obtaining a livelihood."

The rules governing contests for the Queensberry Cups are thus given by Mr. Ned Donnelly, who has taught more winners in these contests than any other professor of the Noble Art—

"1. Competitors to box in a roped ring 24ft. square.

2. Competitors to box in light boots or shoes (without spikes), or in socks.

3. Weights to be—light, not exceeding 10st.; middle, not exceeding 11st. 4lbs.; heavy, any weight. Competitors to weigh on the day of competition.

4. The judging to be in the hands of three judges, whose decision in all cases shall be final. A timekeeper shall also be appointed.

5. In all open competitions the number of rounds to be contested shall be three. The duration of the first two rounds shall be three minutes, and of

the final round four minutes, and the interval between each round shall be one minute.

6. In all competitions, any competitor failing to come up when time is called shall lose the bout.

7. Competitors to draw and weigh on the day of competition. Whenever a competitor draws a bye, he shall be bound to spar such bye for the specified time, and with such opponent as the judges may approve.

8. Each competitor shall be entitled to the assistance of one second only, and no advice or coaching shall be given to any competitor by his second, or by any other person, during the progress of any round.

9. The judges may caution or disqualify a competitor for infringing rules, or stop a round in the event of either man being knocked down; provided that the stopping of either of the first two rounds shall not disqualify any competitor from competing in the final round. And they may order a further round, limited to two minutes, should they think it necessary.

10. In all competitions the decision shall be given in favour of the competitor who displays the best style, and obtains the greatest number of points. The points shall be—for 'Attack,' direct clean hits with the knuckles of either hand, on

DEFINITIONS AND RULES.   359

any part of the front or sides of the head or body above the belt; 'Defence,' guarding, slipping, ducking, counter-hitting, or getting away. Where points are otherwise equal, consideration to be given to the man who does the most of the leading off.

11. The judges may, after cautioning the offender, disqualify a competitor who is boxing unfairly, by flicking or hitting with the open glove, by hitting with the inside or butt of the hand, the wrist, or elbow, or by wrestling, or roughing at the ropes.

12. In the event of any question arising not provided for in these rules, the judges and referee to have full power to decide such question or interpretation of rule."

There are several other quotations or interpretations of the Queensberry Rules—one set for endurance contests, and another for ordinary three-round competitions. Most of the professional glove contests of recent years are supposed to have been governed by one or other set of Queensberry Rules.

Many of the rules of the Amateur Boxing Association are similar to the above, but they have further details as to the size of ring, weights, etc. The first rule, for example, says that in all open competitions the ring shall be roped, and " not less than 12ft. or more than 24ft. square." This is a big difference, one ring being just four times the size of the other. Then there is the question of the correct garments to be worn; and the weights of competitors, not, as the late Mr. Sampson of the *Referee* jokingly said, "for every half-pound above the weight of an Ostend rabbit," but from the "Bantam" at 8st. 4lbs. and under, to the middle weight of 11st. 4lbs. That is to say, we have the

    "Bantam," 8st. 4lbs.
    "Feather," 9st. 0lbs.
    "Light," 10st. 0lbs.
    "Middle," 11st. 4lbs.
    "Heavy," any weight.

Thus a man of any weight can enter for heavies; a "bantam," "feather," or "light" for "middles," a "bantam" or "feather" for the "light," and so on.

The interpretation of many of the rules must be left to the discretion of the judges, who will often have some difficulty in deciding nice points which are always liable to come up for settlement.

It will perhaps be as well to give the rules of the Amateur Boxing Association, *in order*, if only for purposes of reference, so here they are—

"1. In all competitions the ring shall be roped

and of not less than 12ft. or more than 24ft. square.

2. Competitors to box in light boots or shoes (without spikes), or in socks, with knickerbockers, breeches or trowsers, and sleeve jerseys.

3. Weights to be—Bantam, not exceeding 8st. 4lbs.; feather, not exceeding 9st.; light, not exceeding 10st.; middle, not exceeding 11st. 4lbs; heavy, any weight. Competitors to weigh on the day of competition in boxing costume, without gloves.

4. In all open competitions the result shall be decided by two judges with a referee. A timekeeper shall be appointed by the judges.

5. In all open competitions the number of rounds to be contested shall be three. The duration of the first two rounds shall be three minutes, and of the final round four minutes, and the interval between each round shall be one minute.

6. In all competitions, any competitor failing to come up when time is called shall lose the bout.

7. Where a competitor draws a bye, such competitor shall be bound to spar such bye for the specified time, and with such opponent as the judges of such competition may approve.

8. Each competitor shall be entitled to the assistance of one second only, and no advice or coaching shall be given to any competitor by his

second, or any other person, during the progress of any round.

9. In all open competitions the result shall be decided by two judges and a referee, who shall be stationed apart. The judges shall award, at the end of each of the first two rounds, five marks, and at the end of the third round seven marks to the best man, and a proportionate number to the other competitor. At the end of each bout the judges' papers are collected by an official appointed for the purpose. In cases where the judges agree, such official shall announce the name of the winner, but in cases where the judges disagree, such official shall so inform the referee, who shall thereupon himself decide.

10. The referee shall have power to give his casting vote when the judges disagree, or to stop a round in the event of either man being knocked down; the stopping of either of the first two rounds shall not disqualify any competitor from competing in the final round. And he can order a further round, limited to two minutes, in the event of the judges disagreeing. In the event of a competitor being knocked down, his opponent shall retire out of distance, and shall not recommence boxing until told to do so by the referee. The referee shall have power to stop a

round if in his opinion a competitor is being too severely punished.

11. That the decision of the judges or referee, as the case may be, shall be final and without appeal.

12. In all competitions the decision shall be given in favour of the competitor who displays the best style, and obtains the greatest number of points. The points shall be for 'Attack,' direct clean hits with the knuckles of either hand on any part of the front or sides of head, or body above the belt; 'defence,' guarding, slipping, ducking, counter-hitting, or getting away. Where points are otherwise equal, consideration to be given to the man who does most of the leading off.

13. The referee may disqualify a competitor for delivering a foul blow, whether intentionally or otherwise, and after cautioning the offender, he may also disqualify any competitor who is boxing unfairly by flicking or hitting with the open glove, by hitting with the inside or 'butt' of the hand, the wrist, shoulder or elbow, or by wrestling, or roughing at the ropes.

14. In the event of any question arising not provided for in these rules, the judges and referee to have full power to decide such question or interpretation of rule."

The latter paragraph is a very necessary one, for

it is quite impossible to frame rules to meet all cases, and the decision of what exactly constitutes, say, "roughing at the ropes" or "slipping down to avoid punishment," must be left to the judgment of the best men procurable. The laws of the land are variously interpreted by even our own judges; "personal error" has to be allowed for in observations with delicate mathematical instruments, and it is not to be wondered at then, where two combatants are *darting* about the ring with great rapidity, no two or three bystanders will receive *quite* the same impression of what is taking place.

To quote once more from the "All England Series," and with the kind permisson of my publishers, Messrs George Bell and Sons—

"What exactly constitutes 'roughing at the ropes' will, it seems to me, always have to be left to the discretion of the judges at each particular contest. It is to be regretted that this should be so, and that judges cannot be provided with a good definition of this particular form of roughing to enable them to know exactly when to disqualify a competitor.

"Take the case of a heavy weight, A, who has been following round the ring a very quick, slippery opponent, B, who is not such a good boxer, but happens to be in rather better condi-

DEFINITIONS AND RULES. 365

tion. We will suppose that A at last succeeds in 'getting at' his opponent—say, in a corner of the ring. If B's leg, or any portion of his person, is in contact with either stakes or ropes, he is, in a sense, 'on the ropes,' though between this position and hanging over in a helpless condition there are many grades.

"The question is this: Is A to wait till B gets clear of the ropes altogether, and so lose the opportunity of putting in his hits; or is he to go in at once and do all the execution he can while he has the chance?

"If he is to take the former course, he is frightfully handicapped, for he has to throw away what may possibly be his only chance of winning; if the latter, he is almost as likely to lose on the score of 'roughing'; for, if B is in contact with the ropes before the final attack, where will he be when the heavier man has come to close quarters with his contracted-arm hits?

"Stakes and ropes have been so long inseparably connected with matters fistic, that they must be regarded as part and parcel of the game, otherwise a raised platform, somewhat larger in area than the twenty-four-foot ring, and unprotected with any barrier save a strong two-foot railing, might be tried; it would be more attended with danger, but would put a stop to a good deal of the rushing style of sparring one sees so much of, and there would be no ropes to rely on as props.

"To say that a man is not to be hit when leaning against the ropes, opens the door to all sorts of trickery worse than going down to avoid punishment; for, with such a rule, any one hard pressed or short of wind has only to lean for a few seconds on the friendly ropes, and thus gain an unfair advantage of an opponent who is justly entitled to a few points.

"To decide fairly upon the moment where the legitimate scoring ends and the unsportsmanlike hammering and bashing on the ropes begins, will probably trouble the judges of future generations as it has those of the present day and those of former years."

If there be any honour and glory attaching to the position of judge or referee, it is certainly deserved, for a more difficult and thankless job it is hard to find.

It is, as we have seen from the above rules, usual to have two judges and a referee. It seems to me that it would be better, though it might be more complicated, if there were four judges and a referee, and I think they should all sit apart. The judges at the centre of the four sides of the ring, and the referee might be perched in some more elevated position, from which he could get the best *general* and comprehensive view of the proceedings.

The timekeeper should only keep time. If he is worried by looking after anything else, he is very liable to miss out or add on a couple of odd minutes here and there. The office of timekeeper was very commonly combined with that of referee in the old days, but it was a mistaken system altogether.

Jack Broughton, who flourished as Champion between 1734 and 1750, must be regarded as one of the chief founders of the art of self-defence. He followed the ancient Figg, but in matters purely "fistic" excelled that worthy in science.

Broughton it was who established the following short Code in 1743, and it is instructive to compare this with the Revised Rules of the Ring governing contests at meetings of the Pugilistic Association more than one hundred years later.

BROUGHTON'S RULES.

" 1. That a square of a yard be chalked in the middle of the stage; and that at every fresh set-to after a fall, or being parted from the rails, each second is to bring his man to the side of the square, and place him opposite the other; and till they are fairly set-to at the lines, it shall not be lawful for the one to strike the other.

2. That, in order to avoid any disputes as to the time a man lies after a fall, if the second does not bring his man to the side of the square within the space of half a minute, he shall be deemed a beaten man.

3. That, in every main battle, no person whatever shall be upon the stage except the principals and their seconds; the same rule to be observed in bye-battles, except that in the latter, Mr. Broughton is allowed to be upon the stage to keep decorum, and to assist gentlemen in getting to their places; provided always that he does not interfere in the battle; and whoever presumes to infringe these rules, to be turned immediately out of the house. Everybody is to quit the stage as soon as the champions are stripped, before they set-to.

4. That no champion be deemed beaten unless he fails coming up to the line in the limited time; or that his own second declares him beaten. No second is to be allowed to ask his man's adversary any questions, or advise him to give out.

5. That, in the bye-battles, the winning man to

DEFINITIONS AND RULES. 369

have two-thirds of the money given, which shall be publicly divided upon the stage, notwithstanding any private agreement to the contrary.

6. That to prevent disputes, in every main battle, the principals shall, on coming on the stage, choose from among the gentlemen present two umpires, who shall absolutely decide all disputes that may arise about the battle; and if the two umpires cannot agree, the said umpires to choose a third, who is to determine it.

7. That no person is to hit his adversary when he is down, or seize him by the ham, the breeches, or any part below the waist: a man on his knees to be reckoned as down."

These rules, though of course inadequate to meet all the later requirements, formed the foundation of our present ideas of manly fair play in the ring.

Waves of degeneracy seem to have swept over and, as it were, temporarily swamped straightforward and manly feeling at intervals of various lengths. The atmosphere of the ring-side has been periodically tainted by the most blackguard and un-English influences which have from time to time brought the Noble Art into sad disfavour. Such evil influences have not, however, held sway for any length of time, and at the present day any approach at unfair play is looked upon with disgust in this country, in the Colonies, and in America.

In the celebrated battle of December 8, 1863, when Tom King defeated Heenan (*see* p. 330), there was a great deal too much "clinching," wrestling, and throwing, and too little display of scientific boxing, though in the end it must be allowed that the straighter hitting of King won for him the day, after a desperate, slashing, and unscientific fight of a little over thirty minutes.

It was felt that the rules of the Ring were, as they then existed, insufficient to meet the various contingencies constantly arising in prize battles, and therefore the members of the Pugilistic Association, acting in concert with the recognized members of the Prize Ring, framed a set of rules which it would be hard to beat in the matter of comprehensiveness and fairness. They are here given because they may be useful for reference, and do not appear to be out of place in a volume like the present.

RULES OF THE RING AS REVISED BY THE PUGILISTIC ASSOCIATION.

"1. That the ring shall be made on turf, and shall be 24ft. square formed of stakes and ropes, the latter extending in double lines, the uppermost line being 4ft. from the ground, and the lower 2ft. from the ground. That in the centre of the ring a mark be formed, to be termed the 'scratch'; and that at two opposite corners, as may be selected, spaces be enclosed by other marks sufficiently large for the reception of the seconds and bottle-holders, to be entitled 'the corners.'

2. That each man shall be attended to the ring by a second and bottle-holder, the former provided with a sponge, and the latter with a bottle of water. That the combatants, on shaking hands, shall retire until the seconds of each have tossed for choice of position, which adjusted, the winner shall choose his corner according to the state of the wind or sun, and conduct his man thereto; the loser taking the opposite corner.

3. That each man shall be provided with a handkerchief of a colour suitable to his own fancy, and that the seconds proceed to entwine these handkerchiefs at the upper end of one of the centre stakes. That these handkerchiefs shall be called 'the colours'; and that the winner of the battle at the conclusion shall be entitled to their possession as the trophy of victory.

4. That two umpires shall be chosen by the

seconds or backers to watch the progress of the battle, and take exception to any breach of the rules hereafter stated. That a referee shall be chosen by the umpires, unless otherwise agreed on, to whom all disputes shall be referred ; and that the decision of this referee, whatever it may be, shall be final and strictly binding on all parties, whether as to the matter in dispute or the issue of the battle. That the umpires shall be provided with a watch for the purpose of calling time; and that they mutually agree upon which this duty shall devolve, the call of that umpire only to be attended to, and no other person whatever to interfere in calling time. That the referee shall withhold all opinion till appealed to by the umpires, and that the umpires strictly abide by his decision without dispute.

5. That on the men being stripped it shall be the duty of the seconds to examine their drawers, and if any objection arise as to insertion of improper substances therein, they shall appeal to their umpires, who, with the concurrence of the referee, shall direct what alterations shall be made.

6. That in future no spikes be used in fighting-boots except those authorized by the Pugilistic Association, which shall not exceed three-eighths of an inch from the sole of the boot, and shall not

be less than one-eighth of an inch broad at the point; and it shall be in the power of the referee to alter, or file in any way he pleases, spikes which shall not accord with the above dimensions, even to filing them away altogether.

7. That both men being ready, each man shall be conducted to that side of the scratch next his corner previously chosen; and the seconds on the one side, and the men on the other, having shaken hands, the former shall immediately return to their corners, and there remain within the prescribed marks till the round be finished, on no pretence whatever approaching their principals during the round, under a penalty of five shillings for each offence, at the option of the referee; the penalty, which will be strictly enforced, to go to the funds of the Association. The principal to be responsible for every fine inflicted on his second.

8. That at the conclusion of the round, when one or both of the men shall be down, the seconds and bottle-holders shall step forward and carry or conduct their principal to his corner, there affording him the necessary assistance, and that no person whatever be permitted to interfere in this duty.

9. That on the expiration of thirty seconds the

umpire appointed shall cry 'Time!' upon which each man shall rise from the knee of his bottle-holder and walk to his own side of the scratch unaided, the seconds and bottle-holders remaining at their corners; and that either man failing so to be at the scratch within eight seconds shall be deemed to have lost the battle. This rule to be strictly adhered to.

10. That on no consideration whatever shall any person be permitted to enter the ring during the battle, nor till it shall have been concluded; and that in the event of such unfair practice, or the ropes or stakes being disturbed or removed, it shall be in the power of the referee to award the victory to that man who in his honest opinion shall have the best of the contest.

11. That the seconds and bottle-holders shall not interfere, advise, or direct the adversary of their principal, and shall refrain from all offensive and irritating expressions, in all respects conducting themselves with order and decorum, and confine themselves to the diligent and careful discharge of their duties to their principals.

12. That in picking up their men, should the seconds or bottle-holders wilfully injure the antagonist of their principal, the latter shall be deemed

to have forfeited the battle on the decision of the referee.

13. That it shall be a fair 'stand-up' fight, and if either man shall wilfully throw himself down without receiving a blow, *whether blows shall have previously been exchanged or not*, he shall be deemed to have lost the battle; but that this rule shall not apply to a man who, in a close, slips down from the grasp of his opponent to avoid punishment, or from obvious accident or weakness.

14. That butting with the head shall be deemed foul, and the party resorting to this practice shall be deemed to have lost the battle.

15. That a blow struck when a man is thrown or down shall be deemed foul. That a man with one knee and one hand on the ground, or with both knees on the ground, shall be deemed down; and a blow given in either of these positions shall be considered foul, providing always that, when in such position, the man so down shall not himself strike or attempt to strike.

16. That a blow struck below the waistband shall be deemed foul, and that, in a close, seizing an antagonist below the waist, by the thigh or otherwise, shall be deemed foul.

17. That all attempts to inflict injury by goug-

ing, or tearing the flesh with the fingers or nails and biting, shall be deemed foul.

18. That kicking, or deliberately falling on an antagonist with the knees or otherwise when down, shall be deemed foul.

19. That all bets shall be paid, as the battle-money, after a fight is awarded.

20. That no person, under any pretence whatever, shall be permitted to approach nearer the ring than 10 ft., with the exception of the umpires and referee, and the persons appointed to take charge of the water or other refreshment for the combatants, who shall take their seats close to the corners selected by the seconds.

21. That due notice shall be given by the stakeholder of the day and place where the battle-money is to be given up, and that he be exonerated from all responsibility upon obeying the direction of the referee; that all parties be strictly bound by these rules; and that in future all articles of agreement for a contest be entered into with a strict and willing adherence to the letter and spirit of these rules.

22. That in the event of magisterial or other interference, or in case of darkness coming on, the referee shall have the power to name the time and

DEFINITIONS AND RULES. 377

place for the next meeting, if possible on the same day, or as soon after as may be.

23. That, should the fight not be decided on the day, all bets shall be drawn, unless the fight shall be resumed the same week, between Sunday and Sunday, in which case the bets shall stand and be decided by the event. The battle-money shall remain in the hands of the stake-holder until fairly won or lost by a fight, unless a draw be mutually agreed upon.

24. That any pugilist voluntarily quitting the ring previous to the deliberate judgment of the referee being obtained, shall be deemed to have lost the fight.

25. That any objection being made by the seconds or umpire the men shall retire to their corners, and there remain until the decision of the appointed authorities shall be obtained; that if pronounced 'foul' the battle shall be at an end; but if 'fair,' 'time' shall be called by the party appointed, and the man absent from the scratch in eight seconds after shall be deemed to have lost the fight. The decision in all cases to be given promptly and irrevocably, for which purpose the umpires and the referee should be invariably close together.

26. That if in a rally at the ropes a man steps outside the ring to avoid his antagonist, or to escape punishment, he shall forfeit the battle.

27. That the use of hard substances, such as stone, or stick, or of resin, in the hand during the battle shall be deemed foul; and that on the requisition of the seconds of either man, the accused shall open his hands for the examination of the referee.

28. That hugging on the ropes shall be deemed foul. That a man held by the neck against the stakes, or upon or against the ropes, shall be considered down, and all interference with him in that position shall be foul. That if a man in any way makes use of the ropes or stakes to aid him in squeezing his adversary he shall be deemed the loser of the battle; and that if a man in a close reaches the ground with his knees his adversary shall immediately loose him or lose the battle.

29. That all stage fights be as nearly as possible in conformity with the foregoing rules."

The above regulations appear to have been well framed, and, though over thirty years old, might do very well, with a few alterations, for the present day. If duly observed they would go very far towards securing really fair upstanding fights.

CHAPTER XXI.

SUMMARY OF MAXIMS.

HINTS on the following will probably have come under the reader's eye in the foregoing chapters; there is, however, no harm in recapitulating some salient points in a short summary.

1. From toeing the scratch to termination of round keep your eyes on those of your opponent.

2. Left toe pointing straight towards your opponent.

3. If momentarily thrown out of this position, return to it on the first opportunity.

4. Keep your mouth shut.

5. Let all the joints be free and easy.

6. Avoid anything approaching rigidity save at the moment of hitting and in clinches or throws.

7. Let the weight be evenly balanced on both feet.

8. Let your "leads" be free, but—
9. Don't over-reach yourself.
10. Use straight hits from the shoulder, and—
11. Bring the full weight of your body into all such hits whenever practicable.
12. Avoid hook hits and all round-arm work, except when at quite close quarters, and then—
13. Bring in the contracted-arm or short-arm hits.
14. Swing the body with the short-arm hit.
15. In all hits, whether at a distance or at close quarters, consider your *hand, wrist, and forearm as one piece*.
16. Always hit, as you would in a real fight) with the true knuckles.
17. All motion, as regards long leads and general hitting, should be imparted through the shoulder and elbow with a spring from the hindermost foot.
18. With short-arm hits it is better to let the elbow remain rigidly at right angles, and work the hit with a swing from the loins and shoulder.
19. Don't hit with the inside of the hand or wrist.
20. Let all head-guards tend to glance the hit off, in preference to receiving it on the guarding arm, but—

SUMMARY OF MAXIMS.

21. With body-guards let the guarding arm be in contact with the body and receive the hit.

22. Pay more attention to guarding the body than the head, but, in doing so, be careful that your hands never are seen below the belt.

23. Keep your "knowledge-box" out of danger by "getting out of reach," "side stepping," "slipping" or "ducking" as the case may be.

24. Remember that the further your hands are from the points you wish to guard the longer they will be in recovering.

25. It is hard to *guard* the head without unduly exposing the body.

26. If the smaller and lighter man, endeavour to exhaust your antagonist by making him run about; but—

27. If the larger and taller, try to corner your adversary, but avoid ducking or slipping tactics as far as possible.

28. Avoid hitting your opponent's forehead, which will damage your knuckles.

29. Aim for the lower portions of the head, *i. e.* the face. The sides of the head and the throat are also excellent, but the point of the jaw is doubtless the best.

30. Avoid clinching and throwing, unless in a

street row you may wish to rapidly dispose of a weaker man, and, even then, a hit will probably do the business more effectively.

31. Keep your temper.

32. Avoid useless running about the ring, and last, but not least, keep your *head*, and do nothing without knowing the reason why.

33. In a competition do as much "leading off" as you can: countering and cross-countering may give you the satisfaction of punishing your opponent, but won't weigh so much with the judges as clean leads and clever attacks.

34. In a competition enter the ring with a confident and elastic step, and shake hands with your adversary as though you were really glad to see him—as indeed you should be.

35. When taking rest between the rounds get into the most comfortable and easy position for free respirations: lie back in the chair, stretch out the legs with the knees straight and far apart, throw the arms across the ropes, and take as much air in as possible with the mouth open.

36. Avoid the use of stimulants except in the event of great prostration, when the mouth may be washed out with brandy or brandy-and-water.

APPENDIX.

LIST OF THE CHAMPIONS OF ENGLAND FROM THE YEAR 1719 TO 1863.

THE vicissitudes and humours of the Prize Ring, from the days when James Figg instructed the "Sports" of his day in "ye use of ye small backsword and quarter-staff at home and abroad," to the times when Tom King lowered the colours of the Benicia Boy, will hardly fail to interest any who have pursued the foregoing pages, and, as mentioned in the Preface, accounts of all noteworthy fights will be found in *Pugilistica* and *Boxiana*.

1719. James Figg, of Thane, Oxfordshire.
1730–1733. Pipes and Gretting (with alternate success).
1734. George Taylor.
1740. Jack Broughton, the Waterman.
1750. Jack Slack, of Norfolk.
1760. Bill Stevens, the Nailor.
1761. George Meggs, of Bristol.
1762. George Millsom, the Baker.
1764. Tom Juchan, the Pavior.
1765–9. Bill Darts.
1769. Lyons, the Waterman.
1771. Peter Corocan (doubtful). He beat Bill Darts, who had previously been defeated by Lyons.
1777. Harry Sellers.
1780. Jack Harris (doubtful).
1783–91. Tom Johnson (Jackling), of York.
1791. Benjamin Brain (Big Ben), of Bristol.
1792. Daniel Mendoza.
1795. John Jackson.
1800–5. Jem Belcher, of Bristol.
1805. Henry Pearce, the "Game Chicken."
1808. John Gully (afterwards M.P. for Pontefract).
1809. Tom Cribb.

1824. Tom Spring.
1825. Jem Ward.
1833. Jem Burke (the "Deaf 'un").
1839. William Thompson ("Bendigo").
1841. Benjamin Caunt.
1845. "Bendigo" beat Caunt and received the belt.
1850. William Perry ("the Tipton Slasher").
1851. Harry Broome.
1857. Tom Sayers.
1860. Tom Sayers (retired after his fight with Heenan, and left the belt for competition).
1861. Jem Mace, of Norwich, still living.
1863. Tom King.
1863. Tom King, who defeated Heenan.

After the last of these fights, legislation began to step in to the great discomfiture of the Prize Ring, and "free agents" were not allowed to break the peace, as it is called, and their friends and admirers were also made liable as spectators. Each *particeps criminis* was, when caught, punishable by law, and people began to feel that the game was not worth the candle. Of the above Champions Jem Mace is the only survivor, and he must be still going strong, since in September of the present year 1897 he was well enough, at the ripe age of sixty-seven, to stand up for three rounds with Mike Donnovan, a much younger man. May all my readers be able to follow old Jem's excellent lead when they so nearly approach threescore years and ten!

www.ingramcontent.com/pod-product-compliance
Ingram Content Group UK Ltd.
Pitfield, Milton Keynes, MK11 3LW, UK
UKHW041952230426
12048UKWH00008B/281